DOMINE DIRIGE NOS

THE CITY

THE CITY

THE TRADITIONS AND POWERFUL PERSONALITIES OF THE WORLD'S GREATEST FINANCIAL CENTRE

Edited, photographed and designed by

Jacques Lowe

Written by

Sandy McLachlan

Researched by

Fiona Pilkington

With a foreword by

Sir Kenneth Cork

A QUARTET/VISUAL ARTS BOOK

A Quartet/Visual Arts Book
First Published 1982
Quartet Books Limited
27/29 Goodge Street, London W1P 1FD

British Library Cataloguing in Publication Data

Lowe, Jacques
The city.
1. London (England) – Description
I. Title   II. McLachlan, Sandy
914.21'204858   DA679

ISBN 0-7043-2346-X

This book is dedicated to the 'spirit' of the City.

CONTENTS

FOREWORD

I don't suppose that anyone watching the Lord Mayor's Show – and these days, through the medium of television, millions do – ever considers the Lord Mayor leaning out through the window of that superb State Coach. The people waving back at the Lord Mayor see him simply as the newest in a long line of officials representing a great city; but in the course of the procession to the Royal Courts of Justice and back to Mansion House, the man in the coach sees a good part of that great city he is fortunate enough to represent.

In the crowds lining the route there are many recognizable faces. The City is not a big place and although many tourists come to watch, so too do the people who live and work there. However grand the Lord Mayor may appear on that day, he knows many of these people because he meets them in everyday life.

He knows too that the procession preceding him is a celebration of centuries of tradition and good common sense. The history of the City is there; the City's government is there; so too are many representatives of the modern business community of the City.

Every year without fail, thousands of people connected with various aspects of City life put in many hours of freely given time to ensure that the day is a success. Perhaps this is one of the reasons why the City itself is such a success. City people are unashamedly proud of their heritage, secure in the knowledge that they are doing a good job in the present and confident that nothing will change that in the future.

The influence of the City extends throughout the world; its code of conduct, based on absolute trust, and its financial institutions are the envy of all. However, at the end of the day, the City itself is still a village. That is one of its great advantages: the affairs of the village are run for the benefit of the village. The people who run it are in close touch with those who live and work in it and very often all three groups overlap. These may be the politics of the parish pump . . . but they have proved to work very well in practice.

Only people like myself, who have been involved with the City in all its aspects for many years, can appreciate how difficult it is to capture the atmosphere of the place in pictures and words. I am happy to say that Jacques Lowe and Sandy McLachlan have achieved that in a way that will delight those who have already spent a lifetime in the City and be a revelation to those who up to now are unfamiliar with the Square Mile.

This book illustrates both the beauty of the City and its business face. But above all it highlights the people; and it has been the people of the City who, for more than a thousand years, have made our City the remarkable place it is today.

We love this City of ours . . . and so will you!

Kenneth Cork

TRADITIONAL CITY

The Square Mile that is the City of London is a self-contained city within a city. It occupies just 677 acres in the heart of a London that has grown to sixty times its original size, yet it has lost neither its character nor its independence. Its origins go back almost two thousand years, and its offices of government, its traditions and its wealth more than a thousand. It retains rights and privileges won or bought from kings or governments over many hundreds of years, and delights in its pomp and ceremony. Yet, in terms of government, the pageantry cloaks one of the most efficient and forward-looking local authorities in Britain; in terms of business, the City is the financial capital of the world.

The story of the City of London today is inextricably linked with its history and is as extraordinary as that history. Fewer than 7,000 people actually live within its boundaries; each working day, more than 350,000 people commute by car, bus or train from up to sixty miles away to work there. They pour out of the railway termini such as Cannon Street, Liverpool Street and Waterloo; they pack like sardines on to London's underground system; they cram their cars into multi-storey carparks, then make their way to banks, broking houses, insurance companies, newspapers and any other type of office one can think of, to resume the daily task of financing and organizing world trade.

These people are the inheritors of a proud business tradition that predates the Norman Invasion in 1066, for London was one of Europe's leading cities even in Roman times. They are also the successors of the great merchants and entrepreneurs of the Middle Ages who created the City's original wealth and, more importantly, used it wisely to purchase freedoms and charters that have since played a major part in allowing the City to retain its financial pre-eminence in a vastly changing world.

Today, there are not many visible signs of the City's ancient history: high-rise buildings dominate the skyline – a few residential, but most commercial – packed with the modern-day communications equipment that is essential when the need arises to make contact in seconds with any of the world's markets. Fragments of the Roman wall remain, however; some Norman architecture has survived the twin perils of fire and redevelopment; and even Saxon remains have been uncovered. Perhaps the greatest bonus from earlier times are the Wren churches, built after the Great Fire of 1666 which destroyed about two-thirds of the then City. Such reminders of the old London do not seem out of place, although they are scattered, apparently at random, among the results of later town planning. Indeed, the City's ability to get the best out of merging old with new is outweighed only by its ability to survive. Since it was founded by the Romans it has been invaded by Britons, Saxons, Danes and Normans; has lived through two great plagues, two great fires, and a civil war. It has overcome endless raids on its coffers by cash-hungry monarchs (sometimes winning concessions in the process – but very often not), yet has always emerged from lean periods, going from strength to strength.

As the City itself has survived, so have its institutions. The right of the City to elect its own Mayor is enshrined in the Magna Carta of 1215; King John's insistence that the successful candidate should be subject to Royal approval holds good even today: the pomp and pageantry of November's Lord Mayor's Show includes the ceremony in which the new Lord Mayor presents himself for approval by the Royal Justices at the Royal Courts of Justice in the Strand.

The links that have always existed between the business and the governmental aspects of the City are as close today as they have ever been. The Lord Mayor is not chosen by the enfranchised electorate but by the liverymen of the City livery companies, who in medieval times were the most powerful mechants. Indeed, until the last century it was necessary to be a member of a livery company in order to become a freeman of the City, and only freemen could vote or stand for office. Now, although the law is less restrictive, custom and practice still dictate that the Lord Mayor, the Sheriffs and Aldermen should be members of livery companies.

Like the livery companies themselves, these offices go back to medieval times, as do appointed offices, such as that of Town Clerk and Chamberlain; so too does the City's elected legislature, the Court of Common Council: just as in the thirteenth century, the City's twenty-five wards still elect one Alderman (effectively for life) and a number of Common Councillors (who stand for re-election each year).

The Court of Common Council runs the Corporation of the City of London; it is the only local authority in the United Kingdom that is not elected along party political lines; it is also the only Corporation to have its own police force. Although many of its ancient privileges are today more ceremonial than real, the City still enjoys a great degree of independence, both as a body of government and in its business activities. Parliament is as reluctant today to interfere with the City's traditional privileges as it was 900 years ago, and the modern financial City of London enjoys a degree of self-regulation that would be regarded as unthinkable in other world business centres.

To the outsider, the City should perhaps be looked on as an ancient but flourishing club. Its membership is extensive, but exclusive; although many of its rules are unwritten, they are binding by tradition. Election to various branches of the club can be hereditary, through the liveries, say, or London's famous banking families – but merit and money are other acceptable qualifications. Traditions and treasures, quirks and ceremonies, all contribute to the clublike atmosphere.

EARLY HISTORY

The history of this club reaches back to the Roman invasion of Britain by Aulus Plautius in A.D. 43. Having forced a crossing of the Thames, Plautius formed a settlement on hilly ground on the north bank . . . and this Roman encampment was the first London.

The site of Roman Londinium meant little to the warring and fragmented British tribes, but it had priceless advantages for the invaders. In those days, the River Thames was much wider than it is today but, using Roman technology, the river was bridgeable at this point. At virtually the same point the tidal limit was reached, and this would assist trading vessels getting to and from the sea.

Thus, while Comulodunum (Colchester) was the Roman military capital, London quickly became the main centre of trade. The first London Bridge was probably constructed (not far from the present site) in A.D. 43, and the Port of London – a key factor in the City's wealth for many centuries, and still a major world port today – was established early during the period of Roman occupation.

By around A.D. 100, London's natural trading advantages, augmented by the Roman military road system which improved access to other parts of Britain, led it to overtake Colchester in importance, but it was still vulnerable to attack. In A.D. 61 it had been invaded and destroyed by the East Anglian tribe of the Iceni, led by the warrior Queen Boudicca (Boadicea). Roughly halfway through the period of Roman occupation, this vulnerability was removed. A fort had already been built at Cripplegate on the north-west boundary, but between A.D. 190 and A.D. 210, the entire City was walled round, under the direction of Clodius Albinus.

Enough of the wall remains today for us to trace its path round the boundaries of the Roman city, and to estimate its dimensions: it was probably up to 20 feet high, and 8 feet thick at the base; it was around 2½ miles long and enclosed an area of about 320 acres. At the time of its building it made London one of the biggest walled cities in Europe. Just 200 years after building it, the Romans departed to guard their beleaguered empire closer to home. But nearly a thousand years later, the wall (with medieval additions) was still an important feature of London life: it represented defence and the limits of the City's power and independence. Today, dragons stand at its boundaries on the major thoroughfares, symbolizing the City's power and independence.

The wall ran from the site of the Tower of London on the east, north to Aldgate and Bishopsgate, then west along London Wall to the fortress of Cripplegate, and south, via Aldersgate and Newgate, to the river just to the east of the modern Blackfriars Bridge. The gates themselves have all gone, but their Saxon names are preserved in modern street-names.

By the fourteenth century, the City had expanded to its present boundaries beyond west and north sections of the wall; however, the financial community remains within the wall's original confines to this day, and the very proximity of the big institutions to one another contributes to the close-knit nature of the financial centre.

Apart from the fragments of wall remaining, there are few obvious signs of Roman London to greet today's casual passer-by. The best-preserved remnants are the foundations of the Temple of Mithras which were uncovered on the site of the banks of the Walbrook, a stream which ran through the centre of the City in Roman times. (The remains have been moved from the original site to make way for rebuilding, and are now to be seen, in constructed form, in the much more modern Queen Victoria Street.)

But both the results of the Second World War bombing and digging foundations for modern buildings have thrown up countless examples of the Roman occupation. There is a good display of Roman artefacts in the City of London Museum, and, since building works are often delayed to allow archaeological investigation, each new find helps give a clearer picture of Roman London.

The Romans left Britain early in the fifth century, and with their departure the City went into a decline. All Europe was in disarray and trade fell off dramatically, lessening the importance of London's port. The warring tribes of Britons, Angles, Saxons and Jutes, who filled the vacuum left by Rome, had little need for a walled city.

But by the early 600s, London had re-emerged as an important Saxon town; from that time on, it has never lost its strategic and economic importance. Saxon buildings have not survived (although some remains have been excavated), but it was during the Saxon period that the foundations were laid both for the City's form of government and for the growth of its economic power.

By the year 604, London's population had converted to Christianity (although it was later to revert to paganism for a while) and the first St Paul's Cathedral was built. At that time, England was a land of many kings and the balance of power ebbed and flowed, but London's importance as a port remained firm. Its position made it an international marketplace of prime importance, accessible not only to trade from Scandinavia and the Baltic in the north but also from the rest of Europe and beyond. The network of long straight roads left by the Romans provided access to other parts of the island, and the City's walls still offered considerable, though not insurmountable, protection against invasion.

London never was the religious centre of England – Canterbury attained and has maintained that distinction – nor did it become the capital of England until much later, the early kings preferring Winchester. But the original City remained the unchallenged centre of trade, with London merchants growing rich on their tolls on exports of tin, wool and hides, and imports of wine, spices and many other luxury commodities.

The City's oldest surviving public office dates from this time: that of Sheriff. He was the 'reeve' (or 'portreeve', because London was a walled city) and he collected taxes on behalf of the king. His rural equivalent was called a 'shire reeve', hence the term, sheriff.

Indeed, at this time London appears to have been treated much as a shire in its own right. Apart from royal tax collection, the City seems to have been largely self-governing: all its freemen were entitled to attend, and take part in, the decision-making process of the folkmoot; while legal problems were thrashed out at the Court of Hustings – which was presided over by prominent citizens with legal knowledge who became known as aldermen.

The growing wealth of Saxon England made it ripe for the picking by fierce Vikings. London, though less vulnerable than most of the country, did not altogether escape. In 851, the wooden City within the walls was razed; twenty years later, the Danes were back again, but this time intent on settling, rather than just raiding. It was left to Alfred of Wessex to fight the Danes to a standstill and re-establish English control of London in 886 when he considerably strengthened the City's defences.

War with the Danes continued on and off until the country was united under the Danish king Canute in 1017. Canute reigned until 1035, and again the City prospered as the capital of a London-based empire that included Denmark and Norway. By this time, Billingsgate, later to become the famous fish-market, was already established as an important wharf on the river, and the port of London was again the main centre for international trade and, as such, attracted not only merchants from abroad but craftsmen as well.

It was a crowded and bustling city. The voice of the City was heard loud in national politics too, and it was already acquiring the reputation of a kingmaker. Right up to the eighteenth century, no ruler in England could feel secure without the backing of the wealth and influence of the City.

From the eleventh century onwards, the story of London is really a tale of two cities. Edward the Confessor built the first abbey at Westminster, and rebuilt the palace there. Since then, Westminster has been the seat of government . . . but there is only one City of London, and the centre of trade and finance has remained obstinately to the east, in and around that original Roman city.

With the Norman Conquest of 1066, the scene seemed set yet again for London to man its walls against an invader, but instead mutual respect prevailed. Originally, William by-passed London, pausing only to burn the unwalled Southwark on the south bank of the Thames (that fate was always befalling Southwark). In return for a charter guaranteeing ancient rights and privileges, the City accepted William – sticklers for protocol in the Square Mile still talk of William as the Norman, not the Conqueror.

William lost little time consolidating his position. The White Tower of the Tower of London was begun in 1068, and is the oldest structure in London to remain virtually in its original form today. It is not, however, a City building: the primary purpose of the Tower was to be an insurance policy for the king in the event of the City's hostility, and many a monarch retreated to the Tower in times of unrest. From the very beginning it was a royal palace, outside the City boundary, and it remains so today. It was Henry III who extended William's original fortress, in the thirteenth century, to the shape that is now so familiar the world over.

The smooth transition of the City from Saxon to Norman rule is, in retrospect, one of the great landmarks of its history. Neither trade nor emerging forms of government were seriously impaired, and ancient London gradually cemented its new position by using its wealth and influence to turn custom and practice into law, by the devious means of buying charters from successive monarchs.

THE EMERGING CITY

Under Norman and Plantagenet kings, the City took on a shape that is still recognizable today. The City's oldest church, St Bartholomew's, was built by the monk Rahere in 1123 as an Augustinian priory and hospital on Smooth Field, a name which has come down to us today as Smithfield. Much of the church still remains, and the modern St Bartholomew's Hospital traces its origins back to the one founded by Rahere. St Thomas's Hospital was founded a little later, in 1213, and, in one of those charitable acts that was the hallmark of medieval London, was bought by the citizens of the City for the treatment of the poor and the sick.

The first London Bridge built of stone was begun in 1176 by Peter de Colechurch. It took thirty-three years to complete, but survived for 665 years, and was replaced only in the last century. For many hundreds of years, London Bridge was the only bridge across the Thames, and the citizens took an understandably proprietorial interest in their bridge. Bequests from wealthy merchants for the care and maintenance of 'the Bridge' were a common occurrence as late as the last years of the seventeenth century. Many of these bequests took the form of land, which of course has grown enormously in value over time; so the present-day City of London Corporation now maintains four bridges – the new London Bridge, Blackfriars Bridge, Southwark Bridge and Tower Bridge –

without any cost to ratepayers or central government, the money coming from the Bridge House Estates Fund, which today has an income of several millions of pounds a year, much of it the result of medieval charity.

Very few medieval buildings remain in the City; with so much wooden construction, fire was a constant hazard, and the Great Fire of 1666 was the most spectacular in a long line of conflagrations. Nevertheless, it is still possible to visualize Norman and Plantagenet London from the records which remain, or just from the present-day names of streets and alleyways, many of which are associated with the crafts and activities, or the ethnic groups, which used to occupy those sites.

Magna Carta tells us that by the year 1215, Smithfield was already an ancient market, but it was also the venue for jousting tournaments. Hence, Giltspur Street gets its name from the resplendent knights who used that route to the joust; Cannon Street's name comes, not from the weapon, but from the candlemakers who used to congregate in that part of the City; while Bread Street, Fish Street and many others indicate where particular trades were concentrated. Old Jewry indicates the area where the Jews congregated, operating as the City's first moneylenders – until they were expelled by Edward I in 1290. Lombard Street, probably the most famous name in world banking, marks the place where the Lombards and other Italian merchants settled and gradually took over the primitive banking function from the Jews.

Other names emphasize the deeply religious nature of the medieval community: Blackfriars, Austin Friars and Carthusian Street are all reminders of the monasteries that were part and parcel of life in the Middle Ages and, in many cases, so remained until their dissolution was ordered by Henry VIII in the sixteenth century. Even today there are over forty churches in the City of London, many of them with ancient origins; more than twenty remain of those built or rebuilt by Sir Christopher Wren after the Great Fire. Wren's masterpiece – and his own epitaph – is of course St Paul's Cathedral. Unlike many of his other churches, St Paul's emerged miraculously unscathed from the 1940 blitz on London, although an area of some sixty acres round it was totally destroyed. Careful planning control by the City authorities has ensured that the cathedral is not overshadowed by modern skyscraper buildings.

The names of the churches indicate their Norman, and in some cases pre-Norman, origins. St Olave's predates the Great Fire, and commemorates the Norwegian, Olaf Haraldsson, who helped free London from the Danes at the beginning of the eleventh century and was later canonized. St Mary-le-Bow in Cheapside is another church with special significance for Londoners: it was a Norman crypt, was rebuilt by Wren and was restored again after damage inflicted during the Second World War. To lay claim to be a 'true Londoner', a cockney, one has to be born within the sound of Bow Bells.

City churches tend to have fascinating histories. For example, the Spanish and Portuguese Synagogue – a relatively modern building in City terms, since it was constructed in 1700 to serve the growing Jewish community around Bevis Marks – was actually built by a Quaker, Joseph Avis, who, it is said, refused any payment for his services.

The Temple Church is a survivor from the twelfth century, and its history is part of the story of the City's growing links with the judiciary in the thirteenth and fourteenth centuries: it was originally the chapel of the Knights Templar who moved to the site, between what is now Fleet Street and the river, during the reign of Henry II. From being rich, proud and successful the Templars went to being unsuccessful and disreputable, but still rich. They were disbanded and their revenues granted to another chivalrous order, the Knights of St John, in 1312. While all this was happening, the legal system of the country was being changed substantially, notably with the practice of law on secular matters being taken out of the hands of the clergy. Groups of lawyers began to congregate in London, and in the reign of Edward I the idea of law universities materialized with the foundation of Lincoln's Inn in 1292.

A short while after this, the Knights of St John leased the Temple premises to lawyers, and out of this arrangement grew two other inns of court: the Inner Temple and the Middle Temple. At about the same time, Gray's Inn was formed, to make up the fourth Inn. Lincoln's Inn, (situated behind what is now the Royal Courts of Justice) and Gray's Inn (further north) were both outside the City boundary, but the Temple fell within the City limits. Nevertheless, the members of the two Temple Inns stoutly maintained their independence; successive Lord Mayors, otherwise absolute rulers within the City boundaries, failed to impose their dominance on the Inner and Middle Temples. The Temple Church still stands inside this haven of the law, where the lawyers conduct their own affairs without external interference.

From Norman times the City has retained the privilege of administering its own justice within its boundaries, and recognition of that tradition is built into the modern British legal system. Within the City the Lord Mayor is the chief magistrate and all the Aldermen are magistrates. There are two magistrates' courts, one in Guildhall, which has been the seat of the City's government for about a thousand years, and the other at Mansion House, the private residence of the Lord Mayor. This latter court has the distinction of being the only one in the country which is held regularly in a private house, and the Lord Mayor himself presides there, when his other business allows.

The most famous court of all is also situated in the City. This is the Central Criminal Court: the principal criminal court in the United Kingdom, universally known as the Old Bailey. The first Old Bailey was built in the sixteenth century and today's building, surmounted by the famous twelve-foot-high statue of Justice – with scales in one hand and sword in the other – dates back to the beginning of the present century. Appropriately, the Old Bailey was built on the site of Newgate Prison which itself occupied the site in one form or another from the eleventh century until 1902, when it was finally pulled down. Today the Old Bailey has twenty-three courts; eight times a year, the Lord Mayor presides over one of them, exercising his role as chief magistrate. When he is absent, the primary seat on the bench in one of the courts is left empty and behind it hangs one of the mayoral swords, representing his overriding authority. The maintenance of the Old Bailey is traditionally looked after and paid for by the City.

But that is running ahead of events. During the Norman and Plantagenet reigns, economic and social changes were taking place that were to dominate the City's history for hundreds of years to come. The growth of the guilds, which were to develop into the enormously powerful City livery companies, had begun.

GUILDS AND GOVERNMENT

The guilds first emerged in Saxon times as religious fraternities, looking after their members in life and, probably more importantly in those early Christian days, in death. Churches and monasteries were the normal meeting-places for these guilds, and charity was high on their list of priorities. As they grew in strength they became synonymous with the government of the City: they elected the Lord Mayor, Sheriffs and Aldermen from their own number, and Common Councillors too, when the Court of Common Council came into formal existence at the end of the thirteenth century.

Throughout their long history, the livery companies have never lost the legacy of these early developments. Although their economic power was eclipsed over the last 300 years, they have continued to flourish, with strong religious links and substantial funds to administer for charitable purposes. The liverymen still select the Lord Mayor, Sheriffs and other senior officials. All the Aldermen, many Common Councillors and a good proportion of the City's electorate are still livery company members.

In the early days, people involved in a common trade used to congregate in the same area of the City, and the tradition soon developed for guilds to become associated with a particular trade or craft. Gradually they began to take charge of their own trade, setting standards and controlling membership. As they grew stronger they began to exercise monopoly powers, and their organization became more structured with a three-tiered system of apprentices, journeymen and masters. The extra rank of liveryman was introduced in the reign of Edward III; the granting of livery status to a company remained a royal prerogative until the sixteenth century when this power was transferred to the City via the Court of Aldermen.

At first, it was the merchant guilds which predominated; gradually, however, the craft guilds overtook them, and it was the latter which were to go on to become the great livery companies and London's effective rulers. Just as the City prospered and was able to buy privileges from the monarch (the right of the City to appoint its own sheriffs was bought from Richard I in 1189, when the king needed money to finance his crusade) so too the individual guilds bought their own charters, confirming their rights to control their own trades and winning other concessions as well: monopolies of their trades, and the privilege of owning land in their own right were two of the most important.

The first recorded charter was that given to the weavers in 1184 by Henry II, while the saddlers received their charter in 1272. However it was during the fourteenth and fifteenth centuries that most of the major companies received their charters, although they had been in existence, and powerfully so, long before then.

Charters were a handy source of revenue to successive monarchs since they brought an immediate lump-sum, plus an additional source of tax revenue. If the king wanted to levy an extra tax on the City, he used the Lord Mayor as tax collector; the Lord Mayor apportioned the tax among the companies, and the companies and their members had to stump up. Charters also gave the monarch a useful means of control: the chartered companies governed their members strictly and were able to enforce occasional royal decrees on pricing policies (for example, to stop innholders profiteering whenever there was a big influx of nobility with their retinues when a parliament was to be held).

However, with a virtual stranglehold on trade in the City through their monopolies, the guilds prospered. They also took their policing duties seriously: they enjoyed the right to search and seize substandard goods within the City limits (and in some cases beyond) and to punish offenders. The punishments were severe: often fines and/or a period in the pillory. There is little doubt that the powers were not infrequently abused to allow the emerging companies to discriminate against foreign goods, but they also served to maintain high standards of workmanship.

From this base the guilds grew stronger and proliferated. Some of the major livery companies were granted charters by Edward III, and many won other privileges in exchange for financing Edward's wars against France. By the early fifteenth century, there were more than a hundred guilds or companies, and the market was saturated. Inevitably, demarcation disputes broke out between guilds in overlapping trades; although the final solution was to merge the related guilds – often in relatively hard times, when the existence of the weakest was threatened – this did not prevent open conflict in the meantime.

There was, anyway, intense rivalry between the major guilds and companies: they were, after all, major factors in political power as well as in trade, and would jockey for position in – sometimes deadly – earnest. Frequently fighting would break out between rivals for order of precedence, and then the Lord Mayor had to step in. The most famous occasion, although by no means the most serious quarrel, was between the Skinners and the Merchant Taylors. This was solved by a celebrated mayoral Judgement of Solomon: the two companies should alternate in precedence each year, unless one of them were providing the Lord Mayor. The places at stake were sixth and seventh, and this medieval conflict was the origin of the modern phrase 'at sixes and sevens'.

It was not until 1515 that the Lord Mayor and the Court of Aldermen finally fixed the order of precedence of the major companies. The placings – which have lasted to this day – reflect the strength and importance of the companies at that time, rather than their age or history. The twelve great livery companies in order of precedence are: Mercers, Grocers, Drapers, Fishmongers, Goldsmiths, Skinners/Merchant Taylors, Haberdashers, Salters, Ironmongers, Vintners and Clothworkers. The Dyers narrowly missed out, and had to be content with being foremost among the lesser companies.

Although the internal bickering lasted for a couple of hundred years, it did not stop the companies, and particularly the great companies, from becoming very rich indeed. Within the liveries themselves the gap between those at the top of the hierarchy and those at the bottom widened considerably. The wealthier members gradually became wholesalers and rich merchants – to the extent that they finally became financiers of trade rather than directly participating in it.

For much of the period of the guilds' heyday, the wool trade was the foundation of England's prosperity with, first, raw wool and, later, woollen cloth the major export commodity. At first the wool merchants financed the wool industry, lending against the security of wool crops (or, in the case of the Crown, customs duty on wool). Later, however, the whole industry was financed on an international basis partially or wholly by credit. The bills owed by reputable debtors became negotiable – at a price – and changed hands, replacing direct barter trading or the movement of actual specie. These were the earliest bills of exchange, and their negotiability the genesis of the accepting houses and the discount market, which play such an important part in the City's modern-day success.

The merchants not only lent money to the king, they put up finance for trading and exploration ventures which, in the early days, were fraught with danger, including piracy, but which laid the foundations for the formation of the great trading companies: the East India Company and the Hudson's Bay Company, which later operated with monopoly rights under Royal Charter.

In those days it was debatable which was riskier: lending to the sovereign (royal default on loans was by no means uncommon), or putting up money for trading ventures. However, the rewards for a successful trading expedition could be substantial. Shrewd or lucky investors got a large return on their capital, while many of the hapless went bankrupt.

The wealthy merchants were free with their money during life and generous with their bequests at their death. Many of the beautiful and valuable treasures which the livery companies cherish today were gifts from rich liverymen. However, few of the really old gold and silver cups and plates remain, since they were treated by the companies as a sort of reserve asset, and melted down to meet bills or royal levies in hard times. Merchants gave money for the maintenance of churches and streets, for the building of Guildhall early in the fifteenth century, and for the upkeep of the bridge. They founded schools and built almshouses for the poor which, at their death, they would often bequeath to their companies, together with revenues to pay for their continuance.

The rich companies flaunted their wealth ostentatiously. Coronations, royal weddings, victorious parades and, increasingly, the Lord Mayor's procession, were celebrated by the companies with great pageantry, each trying to outdo its rivals in the splendour of its floats. Feasts were another integral part of livery company life, and the liverymen and their guests ate and drank prodigiously from tables copiously laden with exotic fare. The most famous feast of all was held in 1607 when the Merchant Taylors spent more than £1,000 to entertain James I and his son, Prince Henry. It is difficult to put the figure in perspective, but less than a hundredth of that amount would have been sufficient to provide a magnificent repast for one hundred people. (It might, however, have been regarded by the company as money well spent, since, as a direct result, the Prince and a number of noblemen and gentlemen in his retinue became freemen of the Merchant Taylors. Livery dinners remain a gastronomic delight for those privileged to be invited, and critics of the livery companies still maintain that, although their economic power may have dwindled, their hospitality to important guests is a real factor in the continuing influence of the City in high places.)

The livery companies were at the peak of their power and wealth under the Tudor monarchs, but the seventeenth century was to herald their eclipse. Although, by and large, the City supported Parliament in the Civil War, its coffers were drained by both sides; and worse was to come. The restoration of the monarchy did little to improve matters for the companies. Although the City welcomed the return of Charles II and the subsequent accession of James II, the later Stuarts did the livery companies few favours. Ancient charters and privileges were revoked, only to be restored after James II had been deposed and William and Mary acceded to the throne.

The City suffered two other body blows in the 1660s. The great plague of 1665 brought trade in London to a virtual standstill, and the Great Fire the following year (which did at least kill the plague) also destroyed between two-thirds and three-quarters of the City. Forty-four out of the fifty-one livery halls were razed, and over 13,000 houses destroyed. Many of the livery companies lost valuables and records, as well as their halls. And, of course, Old St Paul's and more than eighty other churches were burnt down. Even the great livery companies were reduced to near bankruptcy.

Although they recovered their financial position and rebuilt their halls, they were destined never to regain their economic supremacy. When the fire of London started in Pudding Lane, the foundation of the Bank of England – to raise a government loan by public subscription – was less than thirty years in the future. New types of financial organizations were in the making; the monopoly and apprenticeship systems which had been at the root of the power of the guilds were crumbling.

The last of the old livery companies to receive a charter was that of the Fanmakers, in 1709; and it was to be exactly 220 years more before the Master Mariners began the trend towards modern livery companies. The Monument, designed by Wren and Robert Hooke to commemorate the fire and built between 1671 and 1677, could equally be seen as heralding the end of a 400-year era of dominance for the guilds and liveries.

But if the livery companies were a spent force in terms of economic power, they were far from finished. The requirement to be a member of a livery company in order to become a freeman of the City continued until 1835 – and then it was the City itself which removed the restriction. Towards the end of the nineteenth century, the livery companies still exercised sufficient political influence in favour of the Tories to cause an irate Gladstone to set up a Royal Commission to investigate them. The liveries emerged from that enquiry relatively well. The Commission took the view that they did a good job as charitable institutions administering the funds at their disposal. Those funds were considerable in 1884, when the Commission reported; they are even more substantial today.

As with the bridge and the City itself, the great livery companies were bequeathed a considerable amount of land by medieval liverymen, sometimes for specific charities, sometimes for general purposes. Even in 1870, the capital value of livery company property was £15 million, according to the 1884 Royal Commission. Today, it must be many times that amount, and the annual income runs into millions of pounds. The bulk of this money is used for charitable purposes. Famous public schools, such as Merchant Taylors and Haberdashers, Oundle (Grocers) and Tonbridge (Skinners), were founded by livery companies or liverymen, but many other, less famous schools also receive support from this quarter, including modern comprehensives. So too do a number of universities and colleges, with the liveries sponsoring chairs, scholarships, awards and grants, and generally putting up money where they feel a need arises outside the scope of the state education system.

Nor do the livery companies ignore their historic links with religious bodies and with care for the poor. Many companies still maintain almshouses or old people's homes, and many a church has benefited from livery company money.

But it would be quite wrong to look on the livery companies simply as anachronistic charity administrators. Today, ninety-three companies 'flourish root and branch' (to use the words from the traditional toast), sixteen of which have received their charters since 1929. The great livery companies with an 800-year history have been joined by Airline Pilots and Navigators, Actuaries, Insurers, Chartered Surveyors, Chartered Accountants and many more.

Some of the ancient companies still retain important rights and duties from their past.

The Goldsmiths still assay gold and silver, stamping items with the symbol of the crowned leopard of Goldsmith's Hall (the origin of the word hallmark); and test the currency each year, in the Trial of the Pyx, to ensure that it has not been debased. Most guns sold in the United Kingdom have been proofed by the Gunmakers Company, and the Fishmongers still inspect the quality of fish sold in the new Billingsgate, just as they did at the old market for many hundreds of years. Until 1912, Stationer's Hall was the only place where one could register copyright on publications, and copyright can still be registered there today.

But the City is as proud of its infusion of new blood as it is of its ancient rights. The formation of companies representing modern financial professions is actively encouraged, and old guilds have adopted modern industries. The Horners, for example, have adopted the plastics industry, and the Fanmakers the heating and ventilating trades.

Unfortunately, none of the original livery halls has survived, although the Merchant Taylors and the Fishmongers are still on their original fourteenth- and fifteenth-century sites. Today, there are thirty-five livery halls, each unique in design and full of the treasures of its company's craft and history. The architecture ranges from seventeenth-century to ultra-modern, with a certain amount of reproduction thrown in. The Master Mariners, fittingly, use a ship moored by the Victoria Embankment as their hall.

Many of the halls are either tucked away in unexpected places or overshadowed by modern glass-and-concrete structures. Nevertheless, they remain a quiet reminder of a system that dominated the City for centuries and that still plays an important role in its government today.

THE LORD MAYOR

At the head of that City government stands the Lord Mayor, who is the chief citizen, the chief magistrate and the head of the City Corporation. Within the boundaries of the City he gives precedence only to the sovereign.

The first recorded Mayor was Henry FitzAylwin in about 1192, whose name appears in documents relating to the raising of the ransom for Richard I (only a couple of years after the City had won the right to appoint its own Sheriffs in exchange for helping to finance the crusade that led to the king's imprisonment). The courtesy title 'Lord Mayor' first appeared in English early in the fifteenth century, although the Latin equivalent, *dominus maior*, was recorded a century earlier.

In the heyday of the livery companies, the Lord Mayor was the undisputed ruler of the City with the Sheriffs and Court of Aldermen. Although the Court of Common Council was officially set up at the end of the thirteenth century and had existed in unofficial form before that, it was not until the end of the seventeenth century that it acquired real power in the administration of City affairs.

Today, the office of Lord Mayor epitomizes the ceremonial grandeur of the City of London. During his year in office, the Lord Mayor is lucky if he enjoys only a few days out of the public eye, for he has to attend a thousand functions and make more than 700 speeches. He can expect to entertain visiting heads of state and make at least two overseas visits himself, as the ambassador of the City and its business community.

For all the ceremonial, the Lord Mayor is a very powerful man indeed. In his year as

Mayor he will meet many thousands of influential people, both within the City and beyond its boundaries. He is in a unique position to canvass the views of the City on any matter which affects it and to pass on these views where they will carry most weight. Few doors are closed to London's Lord Mayor, and he is the spokesman for one of the strongest pressure-groups in the world.

The actual election of the Lord Mayor is an elaborated acted-out charade, since the choice has already been made several years in advance and the line of succession can be predicted. This is never admitted officially, however, as the City can, and very occasionally does, pass over a candidate in line.

The formal choice is made by the liverymen in Common Hall who choose two candidates from those eligible, then the Court of Aldermen makes the final decision between the two. This ceremony takes place in Guildhall on Michaelmas Day, and about six weeks later on the second Friday in November, the Lord Mayor elect returns to Guildhall to take over from the outgoing Lord Mayor in what is known as the Silent Ceremony, since no words are spoken. It is a moving ceremony, and just about the last moment of peace and quiet the new Lord Mayor will get for twelve months.

The mayoral year begins in earnest on the following day, with the Lord Mayor's procession to the Royal Courts of Justice where he is sworn in as Chief Magistrate. This, to Londoners and tourists alike, is the Lord Mayor's Show. Over 150 floats, bands, vintage cars and buses, horse-drawn carriages and marching detachments precede the Lord Mayor through the streets of the City in a carnival atmosphere.

The highlight of the procession, which takes more than half an hour to pass by, is the Lord Mayor in his gilded State Coach, which dates back to 1757. The magnificent coach is drawn by six equally magnificent shire-horses lent by Whitbread's Brewery, which still uses them to pull its drays daily through the City. The coach is escorted by the Company of Pikemen and Musketeers of the Honourable Artillery Company wearing seventeenth-century uniforms. The H.A.C. is Britain's oldest regiment which traces its history back to the Middle Ages – long before it was given a charter by Henry VIII in 1537 – and has always had close links with the City.

The procession makes its way from Guildhall up to the Mansion House and then along Cheapside, past St Paul's (where the Lord Mayor is greeted by the Dean and Chapter of the Cathedral) and then via Fleet Street to the Strand. The return journey is made along the Embankment and Queen Victoria Street, back to Mansion House. Whatever the weather, the whole route is lined with cheering crowds.

As the procession makes its way along Queen Victoria Street, it passes a seventeenth-century building which contrasts with the surrounding Victorian and modern buildings. This is the College of Arms, the arbiter on heraldic matters since at least the fifteenth century; here, the three Kings of Arms, the six Heralds and the four Pursuivants decide on grants of arms and other genealogical and heraldic matters. It would have been here that the City's own armorial bearings were considered and approved. First mention of the City's crest was made in 1381 but, in its present form, the City's coat of arms dates from 1609. The City Shield, with the Sword of St Paul in its top left quarter, is supported by the City's two dragons. Underneath is the City motto: *Domine dirige nos* – 'Lord guide us'.

When the State Coach arrives back at Mansion House, the Lord Mayor is home. This opulently appointed building was constructed by the City for its Lord Mayors in the eighteenth century, completed in 1753. The glittering Egyptian Hall is the scene of much colourful entertainment, although state banquets are usually held in Guildhall.

Apart from the Mansion House's domestic staff, the Lord Mayor has a private secretary, who himself has a staff of seven, and three esquires, who also double up as ceremonial officers (the Swordbearer, the Common Cryer and Serjeant-at-Arms who carries the mace) and the City Marshal, who was first appointed by Elizabeth I and was charged with maintaining order in the City. Whenever the Lord Mayor attends an engagement, one of the esquires always accompanies him; when they are not on ceremonial duties, they attend to the details of the Lord Mayor's crowded diary, making sure that correct protocol is observed and giving him any briefings which may be necessary.

The new Lord Mayor has not been in Mansion House for longer than a couple of days before the next big occasion of his mayoral year: the Lord Mayor's Banquet. This has been held in Guildhall since 1501; technically, it is given in honour of the outgoing Lord Mayor. It is an important occasion for the future none the less, giving some indication of how the prestige of the Lord Mayor and the power of the City work in practice.

If the Lord Mayor's Show is for the people, the banquet is for the powerful. Those who run the City and the City's business congregate in the Great Hall of ancient Guildhall, watched by the City's two mythical giants, Gog and Magog, and by the statues of famous English statesmen: Pitt the Elder, Wellington, Churchill. They come to hear the Prime Minister who traditionally makes a major policy speech on this occasion, and the Lord Mayor who announces the themes he proposes to follow in his year of office. One of these will be a favourite charity, since charitable work features largely in any Lord Mayor's list of engagements; but, with the Prime Minister a captive audience, there are usually a few remarks, courteously delivered but pithy, about what exactly the City thinks the government should be doing in its interests. The Lord Chancellor as head of the judiciary and the Archbishop of Canterbury representing the Church are also present, and the rest of the guest-list reads like a *Who's Who in Business*.

This is the sort of pulling power the Lord Mayor has, and there will be other chances during his year of office for similar top-level feasts. When there is an official visit by a foreign head of state, it is usual for a Lord Mayor's banquet to follow hard on the heels of the welcoming banquet given by the sovereign. At such a banquet, guests are likely to include the Master of the Rolls, the Chief of the Naval Staff, the Chief of the General Staff, the Solicitor General, the Lord Chief Justice of England, the Lord Chamberlain, along with Aldermen, royalty, ambassadors and captains of industry. On such occasions, great care is taken to ensure that the Lord Mayor sells the City hard, without cutting across the lines of government foreign policy. Courteous public criticism of restrictive international trading practices is not unknown – and one can only speculate how much more firmly such views are put across in private. One thing is certain: the Lord Mayor will be well aware of the trading interests of his constituents. He could hardly fail to be so. In the course of getting to be Lord Mayor in the first place – which involves becoming first an Alderman and then a Sheriff – he will have met many of the City's most important people. By the end of his mayoral year, it would be surprising if he had not met all of them; certainly, he will have dined with all the livery companies, and there is virtually a guaranteed *ex-officio* invitation to the major functions of the business community.

Apart from this, he will certainly be wealthy in his own right – and influential too. Costs of the Lord Mayor's Show, state banquets and certain other functions are met out of what is called City Cash: income from property and other resources owned by the City as a result of bequests similar to those made for the bridge and to the livery companies; but to do his job properly, a modern Lord Mayor is unlikely to see any change out of £60,000 or more in the course of his year in office, money that has to be found from his own purse. On top of that, he will have made a substantial investment in time: the duties of Aldermen and Sheriffs are onerous enough, but being Lord Mayor is rather more than a full-time job in itself.

Such considerations bring the criticism that the City is undemocratic. Demonstrably, the job of Lord Mayor is not open to all. The most famous incumbent of the post, Richard Whittington, was not in fact a poor boy with his cat coming to London to seek his fortune; he was an extremely prosperous member of the Mercers Company, was twice Mayor (in 1397 and 1406), and Lord Mayor in 1419. He was also one of the City's most generous benefactors, contributing to the cost of building Guildhall, setting up a hostel for fallen women, leaving money to the Crown and his own Company, contributing to the cost of piping fresh water to the City (a constant problem before modern sanitation), and to many other good causes. The story also exists that he tore up and burnt notes worth £60,000, owed to him by Henry V.

Whittington may have been more flamboyant than most, but he is typical of the commitment to public service which is characteristic of the City and its Lord Mayors. The City can argue, with a considerable weight of evidence behind it, that the system may not be democratic but that it has worked well for little short of 900 years. There have been many well-known Lord Mayors with few bad ones; nor has the retention of ancient customs and traditions prevented the modern City from competing freely in world markets – and winning. The City would argue, rather, that the process has worked well in its favour.

MANSION HOUSE

The Lord Mayor's coach normally appears only once a year
for the Lord Mayor's Show and is otherwise kept at the Museum of London.

The Sword Bearer Lt. Col. Peter Milo, the Mace Bearer St John Brooke-Johnson, M.B.E., M.A. and the City Marshall Col. John Howard at Mansion House. The two bearers precede the Lord Mayor at all formal occasions.

It was not until the eighteenth century that the City built a permanent residence for its Lord Mayor, but when it did so it did it with style. The opulent accommodation inside Mansion House is not just the Lord Mayor's home for a year; it is the venue for much of the City's hospitality. Guests range from visiting prime ministers to supporters of the Lord Mayor's favourite charities.

The splendidly ornate Egyptian room can accommodate 320 diners. Mansion House maintains a total domestic staff of sixteen, under the direction of the housekeeper and the steward. There are three footmen, three platemen, one gentleman usher of the hall and nine house maids.

The Salon at Mansion House.

The Steward, Peter Drury, and Senior Footman, Hans
Neilson, in the Egyptian room with a silver setting for two.
Mr Drury has served Mansion House under twenty-three
Lord Mayors.

THE LORD MAYOR'S SHOW

Maj. Gen. John Stanyer, C.B.E., Hon. Colonel Commandant, Royal Army Ordnance Corps.

Each November, the day after the election of the new Lord Mayor, the Lord Mayor's Show confirms his reign.

Over 4,000 people take part in the one and three-quarter-mile-long procession and many more come to cheer.

But behind the pageantry lies a serious purpose. The Magna Carta of 1215 confirmed the right of the City to elect its own Mayor, but King John insisted that the nominees should be subject to Royal assent. That still holds good today and the reason for the Lord Mayor's procession is his acceptance on the Sovereign's behalf by the justices of the Royal Court of Justice in the Strand.

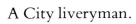
A City liveryman.

M Company 42 Commando
of the Royal Marines in Arctic
battledress.

Royal Marines pass
Mansion House.

The band of the Grenadier Guards passes the Royal Exchange.

A trooper of the Blues and Royals.

The mounted escort of the Blues and Royals approaches St Paul's Cathedral.

Aldermen, City liverymen, coachmen and the beautiful horses and coaches await the Lord Mayor's return from his appointment at the Royal Court of Justice.

GUILDHALL

Guildhall banquet for a visiting head of state.

A meeting of the Court of Common Council, presided over by the Lord Mayor.

Ancient Guildhall is at the centre of the City's government, and has been for a thousand years. The City's most famous Mayor, Dick Whittington, was one of many liverymen who contributed to the cost of the original fifteenth-century building on the present site. The modern much extended Guildhall houses most of the City's civil servants, and accommodates the twice-monthly meeting of the City's governing body: the Court of Common Council. It is best known, however, for its pageantry. It is here that the Lord Mayor and Sheriffs are elected, the Lord Mayor's banquet is held each year at which the Prime Minister of the time is the main speaker, and the City entertains visiting heads of state and foreign royalty.

TOWER OF LONDON

St Edward's Crown with which the Sovereign is crowned. The Sceptre with the
Cross or 'Ensign of Kingly Power and Justice' was altered in this century through the addition
of the great diamond weighing 530 carats and presented by the government of the Colony of
Transvaal to King Edward VII. At right: Queen Elizabeth the Queen Mother's
Crown which incorporates the great Koh–I–Noor diamond. Legend has it that the stone
brings bad luck to men and therefore the crown is worn only by queens.

The Crown Jewels are kept at Jewel House in the Tower. Most of the treasures are connected
with the coronations of kings and queens and almost all date back to the seventeenth century or
later.

Strictly speaking, the Tower of London is not part of the City of London since it is a Royal
Palace and has been since William the Conqueror had the White Tower constructed more to
protect himself from the citizens of London than to protect the City from other invaders.
It would, however, be churlish to dwell on that technicality. The Tower, with its splendidly
attired Yeomen of the Guard, its unique position as the home of the Crown Jewels, and all the
rest of its pageantry and history, is now regarded as an integral part of the City.

Tower Bridge, also just outside the City boundaries, is owned and maintained by the City
Corporation. It is one of four bridges across the Thames which the City pays for out of funds
originally donated by wealthy citizens for the upkeep of London Bridge.

◄ Yeomen (nicknamed Beefeaters) are chosen from ex–military non–commissioned officers with
long service and a good record. Their colourful uniforms are tailor-fitted to each man. The
blue-trimmed uniform is worn every day and this special dress uniform normally only four
times a year, this occasion being the Queen's Birthday.

The Honourable Artillery Company ►
has the privilege of firing
salutes from the Tower for the
Sovereign, visiting royalty and heads
of state. The number
of rounds fired varies. A sixty-two gun
salute is fired on anniversaries
connected with the British Sovereign:
twenty-one for a royal salute, twenty
because it is fired from a royal palace
and twenty-one to express the loyalty
of the City to the Crown. Forty-one
guns are fired for state visits, the state
opening of Parliament and royal
births.

HONOURABLE ARTILLERY COMPANY

R.S.M. J. Campbell of the Grenadier Guards, attached to the H.A.C.

Lt. William Hunt in Gunner Blues, Commanding Officer Lt. Col. Richard Burford, T.D., wearing mess kit and Lt. Mark Huleatt-James in No. 1 dress ceremonial (Infantry).

Non-commissioned officers in the uniform of the Corps of Drums, combat dress, greatcoat order and barrack dress.

Musketeer and Pikeman

The Regimental Colonel, Col. Clive Martin, O.B.E., T.D., takes a salute.

The Honourable Artillery Company is the oldest regiment in Britain and the senior regiment in the Territorial Army. The H.A.C. traces its origins back to 1537 when Henry VIII granted a Charter of Incorporation to the Fraternity of St George, a guild of archers and hand-gunners which eventually became the Artillery Company.

Her Majesty the Queen is Captain General of the H.A.C., and the company's close links with the City are emphasized by the fact that the Lord Mayor, the City Recorder, Aldermen and Sheriffs are all *ex-officio* members of the Court of Assistants which governs the company. In turn the Company's Pikemen and Musketeers form the personal bodyguard of the Lord Mayor.

The H.A.C. has had its headquarters in City Road since 1641 and Artillery Garden is known as the home of the first recorded cricket game in 1725 – fifteen years earlier than the Hampshire village of Hambledon, usually regarded as the 'nursery of cricket'. The first 'aerial traveller in the English atmosphere', Vincenzo Lunardi, also made his ascent from there on 15 September 1784. The H.A.C. performs many ceremonial duties, but as a fighting unit the company forms a part of the British Army of the Rhine and regularly takes part in NATO exercises.

The Artillery Garden is used for parades and drills, but more often soccer, hockey and rugby games are played here simultaneously. In the appropriate season cricket dominates the weekends.

COLLEGE OF ARMS

Keith Evans, the Clerk of the Records, is responsible for entering the full text of every grant of armorial bearings made by the Kings of Arms, for engrossing the letters patent by which these grants are made and for engrossing family pedigrees into the official Books of Record of the College. He also registers other documents, such as royal warrants. Here he studies a scroll of a family's genealogy which he has planned and penned.

◄Michael MacLagan, Richmond Herald, is named after the Honour of Richmond, although his office and function are not local. His appointment dates back to the 1420s and the Badge of Richmond Herald is a combination of the red rose of Lancaster and the white rose of York *en soleil*. Here, in the White Library at the College of Arms, he wears a magnificent tabard of the Royal Arms, normally worn only twice a year: at the Garter Ceremony at Windsor Castle in the presence of the Sovereign and at the state opening of Parliament.

The coat of arms of the College of Arms features the cross of St George, the patron saint of England, which also appears in the arms of the City of London, flanked by four doves, symbolizing the role of a Herald as messenger or, in today's terms, as 'communicator'.

In 1484, Richard III established the College of Arms by a charter of incorporation, giving the Kings of Arms and Heralds a place to meet and keep their records and documents, in a house in the City of London which had been the residence of John Poultney, four times Mayor of London in the fourteenth century and also of Henry V as Prince of Wales. This was located at what is now 89 Upper Thames Street, only a few hundred yards from the present College.

A later royal charter in 1555 – Henry VII having cancelled the earlier one – established the College at its present site, although rebuilt after the Great Fire.

There are three Kings of Arms, six Heralds and four Pursuivants. The Garter King of Arms is the principal King of Arms, with the other two 'Kings' having their jurisdictions as grantees of armorial bearings north and south of the river Trent – Norroy the north, and Clarenceux the south. All are members of the royal household and are appointed by the Sovereign.

The Coat of Arms of the College of Arms.

Since Norman times the Officers of Arms have dealt with armory, shields of arms, crests and heraldic badges and they have exercised the authority to grant, design and assign armorial bearings since the fifteenth century. Today roughly 150 grants are made every year.

While the College's location in the City is incidental, the College has in fact become a City institution in that City men, merchants, liverymen, Sheriffs and Aldermen have always been prominent among those receiving armorial bearings and for over 500 years a close connection has existed between the officers of the College and the senior members of the Corporation of London. From the earliest times Heralds have been members of various City livery companies and a strong link exists between the College of Arms and the Company of Scriveners.

The Most Noble Order of the Garter is England's premier order of knighthood. The ▶ motto of the Order is 'Honi soit qui mal y pense' or 'Evil be to him who evil thinks'. Lt. Col. Colin Cole, Garter Principal King of Arms, is the 34th in succession since 1484. He is a member of the Court of Common Council since 1964, a former Sheriff, a former Master of the Company of Scriveners and a member of several City livery companies as well as a member of the Court of Assistants of the Honourable Artillery Company.

ST PAUL'S CATHEDRAL

A cathedral has been standing on this site since the year A.D. 604, but the present magnificent structure is the crowning achievement of Sir Christopher Wren, the brilliant seventeenth-century architect, who, following the Great Fire of London in 1666, designed and built fifty other churches in the City, most of which still stand. Today he is buried at St Paul's and the words on his tomb aptly read 'If you seek his monument, look around you.'

St Paul's Cathedral took thirty-five years to complete, and as an engineering feat the church is unsurpassed. The great dome alone weighs in excess of 65,000 tons.

Since its completion, the cathedral has served, together with Westminster Abbey, many great state occasions. The state funerals of Lord Nelson and the Duke of Wellington took place here; in modern times the state funeral of Sir Winston Churchill and the marriage of H.R.H. the Prince of Wales, as seen by millions on television, are vividly remembered.

The cathedral's survival of the Blitz during the Second World War can only be called miraculous and made a large impact on the morale of the people of London.

Dean Alan Webster and Residentiary Canons of St Paul's.

53

Although as many as two million tourists visit St Paul's Cathedral a year, this is very much a House of God. Regular services are held daily and on Sundays up to 2,000 worshippers fill the cathedral. St Paul's is the mother church of the Diocese of London and one of its Canons is the Archdeacon of London. Priests and deacons are ordained, bishops consecrated at the cathedral, and hundreds of lay people confirmed each year.

The crypt, here showing military tombstones with Lord Nelson's tomb (originally meant for Cardinal Wolsey until he fell out of favour and coveted by Henry VIII and Anne Boleyn) in the centre, is the burial ground for many men of great achievement. Aside from the many military notables, poets, scientists and writers who are remembered here, Painters' Corner is the final resting place for Sir Joshua Reynolds and J.M.W. Turner.

An army of workmen, some practising crafts long forgotten such as carving wood and decorative masonry, serve the upkeep of the cathedral.

◄ St Paul's librarian Frank Atkinson presides over a magnificent library tucked away in the tower of the cathedral. Its thousands of ancient leather-bound volumes cover the secular and religious aspects of St Paul's Cathedral and include most of the writings, drawings and sketches of Sir Christopher Wren.

St Paul's Choir School

Music has always been an integral part of Christian services, and the St Paul's Cathedral Choir is rightfully considered to be among the world's best. A choir of men and boys has sung daily services for more than 900 years and St Paul's has maintained its own choir school since at least the twelfth century.

Today St Paul's Cathedral Choir School is maintained solely for its choristers, who number thirty-eight at any one time. The boys are chosen through Britain-wide entrance examinations, which include musical, vocal and academic tests. They generally enter the school at the age of eight and leave at thirteen-and-a-half. While boarding at the school, they sing regularly in nine services a week, rehearse roughly nine hours a week, must play at least one instrument – most play two – and undergo a regular academic training programme.

THE CITY LIVERY COMPANIES

A member of a City livery company is also a freeman of the City, a privilege as
ancient as the guilds themselves. In medieval times freemen had special rights and privileges: they
could walk a herd of goats across London Bridge without paying any tax; they were allowed to vote;
following criminal conviction, they were allowed their choice of execution; and if visited by hard
times, they could claim shelter and food from the City. Much of this still holds true today, including
the right to education for one's children at one of the City schools.

To be admitted a freeman today is a privilege accorded to few, but it can be achieved in four different
ways: by patrimony, servitude, redemption and presentation. Currently, the most common way is
patrimony, the automatic right of the son or daughter to take up the Freedom of the Company to which
the father has been admitted. Servitude entails apprenticeship in the original trade or craft that the guild
represents and gains automatic admission. Redemption is simply the buying of one's freedom, but, as
with any exclusive club, the ability to pay is much less vital than the candidate's acceptability.
Presentation is an honorary gift of membership, rarely offered and jealously guarded by all the guilds.

Here a freeman is admitted to the premier City Livery Company, the Mercers, in the presence of the
Master, the Wardens, the Clerk and Assistant Clerk.

The Worshipful Company of Mercers. No. 1

The Mercers' Company, unlike most City livery companies, has never had a strong identification with a craft. The name derives from the French word for merchant and the Company was prominent in the trade in wool, clothes and luxury fabrics such as silk or velvet. Through some of its prominent early members the Company has also been associated with finance and trade in a wider context, for example the founding of the Royal Exchange in 1566 by Sir Thomas Gresham and the later opening of the Bank of England for business at Mercers' Hall in 1694 with a staff of nineteen.

In the reign of Richard II an ordinance was issued requiring all Masters and Wardens of 'all Guilds and Fraternities' to reveal 'the manner and nature of their foundations'. Since then the Mercers have been recognized as Number One among the Companies.

From the early fifteenth century and the bequests of one of its best-known members, Dick Whittington, the Company's identification with charitable works has been strong and its donations and grants have put the Company in the forefront of the City's charitable activities. Today, St Paul's School and St Paul's School for Girls, almshouses in Norfolk and London and Trinity Hospital in Greenwich are but a few of the institutions owing their existence to the Mercers' Company, and the management of charitable trusts is the Company's major concern.

Here the Visitation Court meets in the Court Room at Trinity Hospital, an annual event taking place on Trinity Monday.

The Worshipful Company of Fishmongers. No. 4

The Fishmongers' Company has existed in some form since before the Norman Conquest; it obtained an early patent from Henry II in 1154. The Company's first Charter was issued by Edward I in 1272 and was followed by twenty-three further charters up to the reign of George VI in 1937.
The Company has had its Hall close to the present site near Billingsgate Market since 1434. Destroyed in the Great Fire, it was rebuilt by Edward Jarman in 1671 and replaced with a new Hall in 1834.
The Company's public interests extend to water pollution problems and a general concern with all forms of fishing and water rights. The Company maintains a public school and administers a variety of trusts.

Here Sir Peter Vanneck, Prime Warden and a former Lord Mayor, is seen with his Barge Master and a
Doggett's winner in the magnificent Great Hall.

The Worshipful Company of Armourers and Brasiers. No. 22

Armourers' Hall stirs up visions of chivalry and knightly warfare; indeed the Fraternity or Guild of St George of the Men of the Mystery of Armourers of the City of London was first instituted by ordinance in 1322. In those days there existed several guilds including repairers of armour, those who forged helmets only and bladesmiths. Eventually all joined into one Company. When the use of armour diminished, the craftsmen turned their skills to working with copper and brass – which brought them into conflict with the Brasiers. In 1708, a Charter was granted by Queen Anne uniting the two guilds.

Armourers' Hall, which dates back to 1346, is the only Hall which escaped both the Great Fire and the Blitz, the flames stopping only yards away in both cases. In 1840 the ageing Hall was pulled down and the present one erected. Here the Master, Kenneth Jones and Renter Warden Col. Harley Archer, are seen in front of the elegant inner stairway.

The Worshipful Company of Apothecaries. No. 58

In medieval times the manufacture and sale of drugs was dominated by the Grocers, as many of the goods used were imported. In 1617, against the opposition of the Grocers, the Apothecaries applied for and were granted their own Charter. Gradually the members of the Society became concerned not only with the manufacture of medicines but also with their prescription, which led to diagnosing patients' ailments. The Apothecaries thus became active in the training of doctors and emerged in the forefront of medical reform. Today, the Society remains active in medical examinations and licensing, and most of its members are eminent physicians and practitioners of the medical and apothecary sciences.

Apothecaries' Hall originally was a Black Friars' Priory. The Society purchased the Hall in 1631, only to see it destroyed in the Great Fire of 1666. The Hall was rebuilt in 1668 along the same lines as the earlier premises. Here the Master, Sir Ronald Gibson R C S, a G.P., is seen with the Senior Warden, Dr Douglas Whittet, a pharmacist, and the Treasurer, Dr Geoffrey Cashell, an ophthalmic surgeon, in the Great Banqueting Hall.

The Honourable Company of Master Mariners. No. 78

The Honourable Company of Master Mariners is the first of the 'new' twentieth-century livery companies. Reverting to the original purpose of the guilds, all members must carry full professional qualifications. Incorporated in 1930 under Royal Charter by George V, the Company was soon followed by other bodies such as the Actuaries Company, the Airpilots and Air Navigators Guild, the Chartered Accountants Company and the Chartered Secretaries and Administrators Company The Company's patron is Her Majesty the Queen and its Admiral H.R.H. the Duke of Edinburgh. Aptly, the Hall is a converted ship, H.Q.S. *Wellington*, moored on the Thames.

The Master, Senior Warden and Immediate Past Master Captains
Nicholas Rutherford, George Miskin and Angus Baber on board the Hall.

THE OLD BAILEY

The gold–leafed Goddess of Justice above the Old Bailey balancing sword and scales
is the only statue of justice in the world not blindfolded. This is to signify that
justice at the Old Bailey 'is not blind'.

Here the permanent Old Bailey Judges, Their Honours Charles Lawson, Q.C., Jack Abdella, T.D., Q.C., Robert Lymbery, Q.C., Brian Gibbens, Q.C., Michael Underhill, Q.C., and Francis Petri are seen in the Great Hall of the Edwardian structure designed by Edward Mountford.

London's Central Criminal Court, better known as the Old Bailey (from the name of the Street on which it stands), has been the location of a Court of Justice since the twelfth century together with Newgate Gaol, and has occupied a proper building since the middle of the sixteenth century.

The present building was inaugurated by Edward VII in 1907 and the entire sum for its construction, a massive £395,000, was raised by the City, as were the costs for the two earlier buildings. When part of the building was destroyed and the rising crime rate and the need for more space made the building somewhat obsolete, the City raised another £7 million in the early 1970s to modernize the facilities.

In fact, the court is the Court of the Corporation of the City of London which pays for all its costs, a sum worth millions a year to the government.

Still, that designation is misleading, for the Old Bailey is perhaps the most illustrious court in the world and handles cases, especially in the criminal area, which are justly celebrated and have become landmarks of criminal justice.

Today, twenty-three courts are in continuous use virtually all year, but it is the No. 1 Court which has seen the trial of the likes of Dr Crippen, who murdered his wife and tried to escape to Canada with his young mistress, Ethelle le Neve; Edith Thompson and Frederick Bywaters who murdered Edith's husband then underwent a trial which still is regular television fare, and lately Peter Sutcliffe, the Yorkshire Ripper. Sex murders, gangland slayings, political crimes and high society peccadillos are all tried at the Old Bailey.

The central chair on the bench in each Court is not occupied by the Judge but is reserved for the Lord Mayor of London. To exercise his right to preside at the Old Bailey, the Lord Mayor processes in state on a number of occasions each year and takes his seat in No. 1 Court.

The Recorder of London, His Honour James Miskin, Q.C., and Common Serjeant, His Honour Judge David Tudor-Price, are the senior permanent Judges at the Old Bailey. The Recorder's office dates back to 1298 and that of the Common Serjeant to 1291.

The additional Old Bailey Judges, all Queen's Counsellors, Derek Grant D.S.O., Edward Sutcliffe, Michael Argyle M.C. and Neil McKinnon.

The Aldermanic Sheriff, Lady Mary Donaldson, was the first lady Sheriff ever elected in the City of London. She is here joined by the Secondary and Under Sheriff and High Bailiff of Southwark, Col. Leonard Thacker (centre) and the Lay Sheriff Anthony Eskenzi. The Aldermanic and Lay Sheriffs are elected annually. The appointment of the Secondary and Under Sheriff by the Court of Aldermen is permanent. He administers the City's affairs in the Old Bailey and his duties include the execution of writs as well as the guidance of each year's newly elected Sheriffs.

MIDDLE TEMPLE

The Inner and Middle Temples are two of London's four Inns of Court, the only two that fall within the City boundaries – in spite of which they are self-administering. It is the Inns of Court that appoint barristers in this country, the name barrister deriving from the fact that successful candidates are literally 'called to the bar' to mark their achievement. The two Inns are quite separate entities, but they share the same grounds, leased to them in perpetuity in 1608 by James I, although the grounds were originally leased to lawyers by the Knights of St John in the fourteenth century. The name 'Temple' derives from the Order of the Knights Templar who occupied the site from the twelfth century until they were dissolved in 1312 and the land and buildings handed over to the Knights of St John. The grounds of the Inner and Middle Temples run from just behind Fleet Street down to the Embankment. They include the original Round Church built by the Templars in the late twelfth century. The whole area is a haven of peace and quiet which belies the fact that it is in the very heart of London's conurbation. The atmosphere is akin to that of an Oxford or Cambridge college, with pupils and benchers strolling at leisure through the grounds surrounded by buildings most of which are steeped in history.

'Call Day' takes place twice a year at each Inn of Court. The candidates here, four ladies and one gentleman face the Court of Elders and sign the register, the only proof of their success, since no certificate is issued.

FINANCIAL CITY

The City today is unquestionably the most powerful financial centre in the world, offering the greatest variety of banking, broking and monetary services to be had anywhere. The amounts of currency and paper which are traded daily are phenomenal, and many of the deals contracted, some on the strength of a telephone call or a handshake alone, are legendary.

Nowhere else in the world, not in New York, Toronto, Tokyo, Paris or Zurich, is it possible to raise huge sums of money overnight, because nowhere else in the world does the same trust exist among a small group of men. Although an army of lawyers and accountants service the City, in many cases they arrive *after* the deal has been made. The City doesn't wait until every 't' is crossed and 'i' dotted; 'its word is its bond' – and that is precisely the City's strength.

It is practically impossible to put exact figures to the City's daily transactions, but suffice it to say that they are millions of pounds per day, and that the earnings of the City, according to the Bank of England, contributed £3,452 million to Britain's balance of payments in 1981, a phenomenal amount when considering that the profit on a transaction is often measured in fractions of a percent.

The City is the centre of the world's bullion market, the world's insurance market, world foreign exchange markets, and the world's shipping market. It plays a leading role in international capital markets, is one of the main centres for commodity trading, and has one of the biggest stock exchanges. Nowhere else in the world is there a centre offering the number and size of financial services that the City of London provides.

How did London build up this modern financial leadership and, indeed, how has it managed to retain it in the face of competition from other world centres? A whole host of reasons and accidents are involved, of which not the least must be that of inheritance. In the seventeenth century, when the first modern financial institutions were developing, London was already at the centre of world trade with strong overseas links, forged by the wool traders and other merchants; because of the importance of London as an international port, the City itself was very cosmopolitan and many overseas traders had a presence there. By this time, the use of bills of exchange was already an established form of payment; the banknote was also developing as the goldsmiths began issuing notes against deposits of bullion held by them; instead of the bullion itself, these notes began to change hands. The joint stock principle was established, and was to grow dramatically as the use of limited liability companies became more popular, and the shares became more marketable with the development of the London Stock Exchange.

The small area covered by London's trading and financial community was and is an important factor in its growth. Sir Thomas Gresham's Royal Exchange, opened by Elizabeth I in 1570, gave merchants and traders in all commodities a central marketplace to operate from; as the markets grew and split up, they still remained physically close together. Internationally, London enjoyed considerable confidence because of the continuity and stability of its government. In the early days, government lay in the hands of people to whom business considerations were paramount; up to the present day, central government has pursued policies designed to interfere as little as possible with the free working of the City in international markets: not only because the City retains an extremely powerful voice at Westminster, but also because the government is always conscious of the importance of foreign exchange earnings to be gained from the activities carried out in the Square Mile.

In the middle of the seventeenth century, business was there to be done, and London started to develop new institutions to handle it. Coincidentally, coffee became a popular drink at around that time, and a large number of coffee shops sprang up in London, particularly around the Royal Exchange. These surroundings were more congenial to the merchants than the floor of the Exchange itself, so gradually they changed from being areas of relaxation and gossip to places where business was done. Merchants in the same line of business naturally tended to congregate in the same coffee house. Since there was no formal marketplace for dealing in stocks or chartering or insuring ships, those wishing to undertake such transactions would make their way to the coffee house where they would be most likely to find people in the business they wanted. It is no accident that insurance at Lloyd's, shipping on the Baltic, and the London Stock Exchange all had their original premises in coffee houses (as, much later, did the London Metal Exchange).

These informal beginnings have had a major and lasting impact on the way that business is done in the City. Since everyone knew just about everyone else, much of the business was done on trust, and the markets were allowed to develop without any external interference. In many ways the situation is little changed today. Although there are Companies Acts and Prevention of Fraud Acts to control the running of business in general, the major City markets are still allowed a great deal of latitude in self-regulation. The Bank of England is in close touch with the regulatory bodies, takes part in discussions about change, and gives 'advice' which can be almost tantamount to royal command, but there is little statutory interference of any kind. This gives London the flexibility to react quickly if there is a need for a new market, or if conditions change in existing markets, and is a powerful weapon in the fight to remain competitive in a fast-altering world.

Equally important to London's trading position today is its 300-year-old tradition of dealing on trust. The Stock Exchange motto: '*Dictum meum pactum*' ('My word is my bond') is generally regarded as holding good for the City as a whole. The motto of the Baltic is virtually the same: 'Our word is our bond'; Lloyd's motto, '*Fidentia*', is probably best translated in this context as 'with the utmost good faith'. In the City, a verbal agreement or handshake has always been regarded as a binding contract in honour if not in law, and this fact is widely respected throughout the world. With so much business now done over the telephone, the old tradition has taken on greater importance with the passage of time. On the strength of a single phone call bankers can raise or make loans running into millions of pounds, and hundreds of millions of pounds' worth of foreign exchange dealings take place in this way every day. Flexibility, speed and absolute confidence are three key factors in the City's continuing success story.

However, while these watchwords were being developed, the City of London had yet to gain its predominant role in world finance. How it did so is a story of wars, revolutions, and empires.

War with France is a recurring theme in the fortunes of the City. The French wars of Edward III secured many privileges for the livery companies which helped finance it; and William III's war against France led to the foundation of the Bank of England. Later, the Napoleonic Wars were to tax, metaphorically and literally, Britain's finances; but they also removed competition to London, with the eclipse of Amsterdam as a financial centre.

THE BANK OF ENGLAND

By the end of the seventeenth century, national banks already existed in some countries, but were looked upon with some suspicion in England. Various attempts to set up a national bank failed until, in 1694, a hard-pressed parliament chartered the Bank of England in exchange for a loan of £1,200,000. The money was raised by public subscription, and one of the privileges extended to the new bank was the right to issue banknotes.

Although the Bank of England was, ironically, the brainchild of a Scotsman, William Paterson, the money raised to found it came from the City of London. Straight away it confirmed the first major role of the 'new' City: that of financing the government. Impersonal marketable securities took the place of private loans to the king from rich merchants and livery companies, but the City had retained the role of funding the National Debt. Because it was financing the government, it is hardly surprising that the Bank of England became the government's bank or, more accurately, banker to the government. It also became the bankers' bank, since other private banks increasingly used Bank of England notes and found it convenient to hold balances of cash at the Bank.

In 1709 the Bank of England was granted a new charter in exchange for more money lent to the government, which effectively prevented the development of joint stock banking in England for more than a hundred years. At that time, the ability to issue notes was crucial: the charter forbade any group of more than six individuals to issue their own notes, so that small, private banks could flourish but could not grow beyond the means of six partners. The Bank, exempt from this control, gained a virtual monopoly of note issue in the City, and by the time its monopoly was finally rescinded in 1833 and deposit banking (lending other people's money rather than printing your own notes) had developed, the Bank's primary position was secure.

THE BANK AND GOVERNMENT

The Bank of England was nationalized in 1946 by the postwar Labour government but, in spite of dire predictions, there was little obvious change as far as the City was concerned: the Bank had long been closely involved with the management of the government's monetary affairs, including the management of the National Debt. Since the formidable Montague Norman became Governor of the Bank in the interwar period, the Governor's voice has always carried a good deal of weight in monetary matters, and nationalization has done nothing to change that. Since the Banking Act of 1979 the Bank has statutory authority over anyone wishing to take deposits from the public.

The long-term government debt is financed (or refinanced as old loans fall due for repayment) through the gilt-edged market. The Bank of England's agent in the market is not a public employee, but the senior partner of a private Stock Exchange firm, Mullens & Company. Market forces ultimately determine the level of long-term interest rates, but the Bank can have a considerable impact on the level of interest rates through the price at which the Government Broker is prepared to buy and sell gilt-edged stocks. Also, the Bank always contrives to have at least one issue at both the long-dated end of the market and the short-dated end which has not been fully subscribed. Thus the Government Broker always has stock he can release on to the market in order to help him control the movement of interest rates.

THE DISCOUNT MARKET

The government's day-to-day needs for money are arranged by the Bank through the weekly issue of Treasury Bills to the discount market; its manipulation of the Treasury Bill issue together with purchase or sale of eligible bank bills and Local Authority Bills are its main weapons in controlling the level of short-term interest rates and the amount of liquidity in the banking system. The detailed mechanism by which the Bank manipulates the money markets is complex and varies, depending on the government's economic policy, among other factors, but the underlying principle – keeping the money market either well supplied with or short of funds – remains unchanged.

There are now twelve members of the London Discount Market Association who enjoy the privilege of going to the Bank of England as lender of last resort. The discount houses maintain close informal links with the Bank; the chairman and deputy chairman of the Association have weekly meetings with either the Governor or Deputy Governor. And as part of the mechanism of the money market, the members of the Association agree to cover the whole of the Treasury Bill tender each week.

It is worth explaining at this stage the various roles of the modern discount market. Call money with the discount houses represents the prime sources of liquidity in the British banking system. Flexibility is provided because if the banks are short of cash they can always call money from the discount houses. The houses are always able to deliver the money immediately because the Bank of England will always rediscount securities held by the houses or will provide money to them under the Bank's lender of last resort facility.

The modern discount market serves three main sectors of the economy. It serves the public sector by its weekly underwriting of the government's Treasury Bill issue, by its ability to make a market not only in Treasury Bills but also in the short-term obligations of local authorities and nationalized industries. The market is also an active investor and dealer in British government and local government bonds. It serves the banking system by being investors and the leading market makers in short term bank obligations – mainly Bankers Acceptances and Certificates of Deposit. It serves the corporate sector by the provision of funds through the indirect medium of the Bank Acceptance and the direct medium of Trade Bill finance. In recent years also the discount market has developed substantial commercial business as market makers and the two largest houses in particular, enjoy a substantial daily turnover of money and securities with the non-bank sector.

The discount market has thus played an integral part in the development of London as a financial centre. Its original role in the financing of world trade for the bill market has developed into a sophisticated system of market making and dealing in fixed interest securities of all kinds, representing both public and private sector debt; another example of the ability of the City of London to adapt to structural changes that have taken place in the economy during the twentieth century.

While the discount houses act as principals, there are other money brokers who specialize in acting as intermediaries – for example between two banks, one of whom is long on sterling and the other of which is short. The biggest companies in this field such as M.W. Marshall and Astley and Pearce maintain large international networks.

Building societies too are active in the money markets. They have total assets of well over £60 billion, and keep between 16 per cent and 19 per cent in readily realizable form. A giant society such as the £10 billion plus Abbey National will have around £350 million on call in the money market when it is due to pay half-yearly interest to depositors.

BANKING

Banking is at the centre of any financial system, and the way that the British banking system has developed through the City has had a profound effect on the way that the City operates today. The early bankers were the goldsmiths in London and other wealthy merchants in the provinces. Rich men in their own right who could be trusted and who had the security facilities to look after other people's wealth became bankers, as a secondary function to their own trade. The IOUs they issued to depositors gradually became banknotes, and the canny merchants began to realize that as long as confidence was maintained they could also lend out part of the deposits, entrusted to them, to others requiring money. But it was not until late in the seventeenth century that banking became a business in its own right and the first City bank was established.

When the Bank of England was founded in 1694 it was just another bank, but the privileges accorded to it in its charter had far-reaching effects. One of the principal by-products was to enhance the importance of the bill-broker: the resources of individual banks limited to six partners could not match the increasing capital sums needed to finance the growing Industrial Revolution, so commercial bills became the main instrument of financing trade. Bill-brokers in the City became a clearing house where the borrowing needs of the industrial north were matched with the surplus funds available in the City itself or from the predominantly rural areas.

The early private banks had no clear idea as to how much liquid resources were required at any one time to meet the likely demands of their customers; anyway, their inability to spread risks made them easy prey to any crisis of confidence. Throughout the eighteenth century and early in the nineteenth century, bank failures were a common occurrence.

It was during this period that the Bank of England began to establish itself as the bankers' bank with an element of responsibility for the well-being of the banking structure. With its greater capitalization, it was better able to withstand financial crises than the smaller banks; although it was still in competition with the private banks, it rescued many of them in times of trouble. The Bank itself was seriously embarrassed by the collapse of the South Sea Bubble in 1720. There was a further major financial crisis in 1825 when, as a result of the collapse of a speculative boom in South American ventures, seventy-three major banks suspended payment, and most of the major London banks had to turn to the Bank of England for cash to see them through the crisis. As a result, many banks decided to lend money on call to the bill-broking houses where the interest rate may have been lower than on longer-term lending, but the money could be regarded as cash, since it was immediately accessible. This allowed the bill-brokers to go into business on their own account, buying in commercial bills themselves to hold until maturity, rather than simply acting as intermediaries between other lenders and borrowers. Shortly after that, the Bank of England decided to grant to certain of these broking houses the facility to discount bills at the Bank. This began the discount-house system, which has played such an important part in the development of London's unique money market. As it developed, the system enhanced flexibility in the banking system and gave the Bank of England a small lever to control the activities of the many banks operating in London; it also provided an important element in ensuring that bills on London remained the prime source of finance for international trade and was an important factor in encouraging foreign banks to open offices in London, long before the development of modern eurocurrency and foreign exchange markets.

THE JOINT STOCK AND CLEARING BANKS

Following the formation of the discount market, the next major development in domestic banking was the growth of joint stock banks which were retail banks set up all over the country; as they grew in size through amalgamation and opening new branches, they became a major financial force and thus, inevitably, involved with the City.

Today the vast bulk of British retail banking rests in the hands of the 'big four' clearing banks: Barclays, Lloyds, National Westminster and Midland. These are virtually all that is left of the 154 joint stock banks and 246 private banks that existed in 1866.

The early development of the clearing system is another typical City example of how initiative and informality paved the way for a highly organized and efficient structure. In the eighteenth century, clerks from each of the London banks used to tour round other banks in the City, presenting cheques for payment and returning to their own banks with the cash. The clerks themselves evolved the system of meeting at a central point – probably a coffee house again – and exchanging cheques. That way they only had to carry cash, equivalent to the balance of the difference between the cheques drawn on each bank. The bankers realized the sense in this. It was safer, because less of their cash was being carried round the streets, and it was more profitable, since they needed to keep less cash lying unproductive in their tills. The banks hired a room for their clerks to clear cheques and, when that became inadequate, built a special clearing house in 1833. Today's clearing house still stands on the same site in Lombard Street, but now most clearing is done by computer.

The joint stock banks won their way into the clearing system in 1854, and then proceeded gradually to absorb the private banks, which had previously opposed them. As the private banks disappeared, so did banknotes other than those issued by the Bank of England, which acquired the status of legal tender in 1833. The Bank Charter Act of 1844 provided that no new banks should have the right of note issue, and any existing bank should lose the right to print its own notes upon merging. Since 1921, when the last private bank disappeared, the Bank of England has been the sole note-issuing authority in England and Wales.

As the joint stock banks amalgamated and the biggest extended their branch network nationwide, it was natural that their head offices should gravitate to the City. But much more important was the fact that so too did their surplus or liquid funds. It is the liquid funds of the clearing banks that provide almost half of the money which the discount houses use to finance their business. On any one day, up to £2,500 million of clearing-bank money will be lodged with the discount houses.

THE MERCHANT BANKS

By the nineteenth century, Britain, via the City, was purveyor of capital by appointment to the world. This era saw the emergence of the merchant banks, a new force in the City. Most were foreign in origin: some of them came as merchants and became international bankers through their overseas connections. Others came as representatives of already existing continental banking families; because of the opportunities in London, the offspring outgrew the parent. Some were wholesale bankers: they had few small accounts but raised loans for governments, loans to finance wars and loans to pay for the export of the Industrial Revolution to other countries.

Many of them are household names today: Rothschilds, Barings, Hambros, Lazards, Schroders and Morgans. Some of them are great banking dynasties. Shortly after the end of the Napoleonic Wars – when England was by no means at the peak of her economic power – it is estimated that in the space of eight years the City raised a total of £52 million in loans for European and South American governments, and it was merchant banking houses that were largely responsible for the underwriting. These banks were able to raise such large sums of money because of their reputation and their contacts, but the banks themselves were small and depended on the flair of individuals and a superb information network in their own specialized geographical markets. The most famous of the merchant bankers was Nathan Rothschild, of the dynasty started in Frankfurt by his father, Mayer Amschel Rothschild. Stories about Nathan, who founded the English branch of the family bank and made it the richest of them all, are legion. He knew about the outcome of the Battle of Waterloo before the British government did, and he reputedly cemented the Rothschild wealth by making a stock market killing out of that knowledge. He raised a £12 million loan for the British government, as well as loans for France, Prussia, Russia, Austria, Brazil, Belgium and Naples.

But if Rothschild is well known as the most flamboyant, he was certainly not alone in audacity. In 1870 J.S. Morgan, one of the founders of Morgan Grenfell, the only major British merchant bank of American origin, infuriated German Chancellor Bismarck by raising a £10 million loan for the French during the Franco-Prussian War. It proved to be a shrewd move: the stock went to a substantial discount on the market, Morgan backed his hunch and bought in as much stock as he could lay his hands on. The stock was redeemed at face value by the French government three years after the Peace of Versailles; years before its due date.

Things did not always go right for the merchant banks in their capacity of issuing houses and underwriters, however. In the famous Baring crisis of 1890, the bank was in danger of defaulting on some of its bills which were about to fall due, having over-committed itself on underwriting Argentine loans which were not taken up by the investing public. A major crisis was averted by the intervention of the Deputy Governor of the Bank of England, William Lidderdale, who, in less than twenty-four hours, mobilized support from the rest of the City banking community to the tune of £10 million. This incident brought Lidderdale great praise and put beyond question the Bank of England's acknowledgement of responsibility for the well-being of the City's banking community.

Spectacular though the merchant banks' issuing activities were, they were not the only important contribution these houses made during the nineteenth century. They came to play a major part in the financing of international trade through the process of 'accepting' commercial bills. They did this simply by writing 'accepted' on a bill, together with the bank's authorization. Once a bill had been accepted by a top-flight merchant bank, it was guaranteed convertible at a bank or at one of the discount houses at the lowest possible discount rate. The merchant banks themselves would hold portfolios of these accepted bills, unloading them on the discount market as their cash demands required.

As the joint stock banks developed in England, overdraft took over from commercial bills as the main means of financing internal trade, so foreign bills became the major component in the discount houses' portfolios: the accepting houses were an important bridge between the financing of international trade and the London money market.

THE ACCEPTING HOUSES

The élite of the merchant banking fraternity remains the accepting houses. The Bank of England clarified the demarcation between the first- and second-line merchant banks when it formed the Accepting Houses Committee in 1914, and invited selected banks to join. There are now sixteen members of the Committee, including S.G. Warburg, one of the few merchant banks to come from virtually nowhere into the top flight of merchant banks in the period since the Second World War. Under the guidance of Sir Siegmund Warburg, the bank prospered rapidly and became a member of the Committee with its acquisition of an existing member, Seligman Brothers. The Bank has strict rules relating to the accepting houses: that they must enjoy the highest possible financial standing goes without saying; they must also be based in the City, and be British-controlled. A seventeenth member of the Association, Arbuthnot Latham, lost its accepting-house status in 1981 when it was taken over by a foreign bank.

Acceptance business still plays an important part in the dealings of the leading merchant banks, but today they are heavily involved in most types of international and domestic finance, including advice on the investment of the vast sums of money which Britain's pension funds and life assurance companies have available.

Because of their long experience and the undoubted prestige attached to being an acceptance house, the top merchant banks are still frequently preferred as lead managers for underwriting in the London eurobond market, be the loan for governments or for major industrial companies. They are also much in demand inside the UK corporate sector, bringing companies to the stock market for the first time, raising new funds for existing public companies (usually by means of a rights issue of shares) and masterminding takeover bids (or the defence against an unwanted bid). The wider body, covering all the institutions who engage in these types of business, is the Issuing Houses Association which has fifty-seven members; but the bulk of business is done by its sixteen accepting house members.

FOREIGN BANKS

At any one time about a quarter of the £3,000 million to £5,000 million call money lodged with the discount houses comes from foreign banks based in the City. That is an indication of one of the advantages of having foreign banks in the City; more importantly, it gives an indication of just how major a presence these banks have within the Square Mile.

Probably the biggest single factor in the City's retention of its prime importance in world financial markets has been its success in persuading foreign banks and securities houses to come to London and operate in London markets, using London's well-established framework, expertise, and communications network. There are now more than 400 foreign banks and securities houses represented in London, including all but five of the world's largest banks. Many, especially Commonwealth and American banks, have been represented since the nineteenth century: the Australia and New Zealand Banking Group has been in London since 1834; Chase Manhattan was the first American arrival in 1887, quickly followed by Guaranty Trust Company of New York, in 1892. The majority, however, banks and securities houses alike, have made their appearance in the last twenty years or so, with the Japanese securities house, Nomura International, one of the first modern arrivals in 1964. By 1981, foreign banks and finance houses in London employed over 32,000 people, nearly ten per cent of the City's entire business population.

In attracting these overseas banks, the City has had one natural factor on its side: its geographical situation. It is a part of Europe and situated between America and Asia; its working day corresponds closely to that of the rest of Europe, and overlaps with both America and Asia.

THE EFFECTS OF THE INDUSTRIAL REVOLUTION

During the early development of the financial institutions the Industrial Revolution was taking place in England. This, together with the building of the British Empire, secured the City's future as the marketplace of the world.

The story of the Industrial Revolution belongs to the Midlands and the north of England, since this was where the deposits of coal and iron ore were, and in Lancashire the climate was right for spinning cotton. Although the action may have been in the north, the money came from or was channelled through the City. It was the City which supplied the cash for the capital-intensive industries which were to make Britain into the workshop of the world for more than a hundred years, and it was the City's bill-brokers who turned promises to pay into money. Liverpool may have grown rich on cotton and Bristol on the trade in slaves and tobacco, but London grew richer still on financing the Industrial Revolution. In so doing, it cemented the second major role that it still performs today: that of banker and financier to British industry. Money raised through the City did not just build the factories and finance the working capital: it paid for the infrastructure: the canals and, subsequently, the railways that were the first major advance in communications since the Romans built their roads.

London reaped a double financial benefit from these developments. It made handsome profits on financial transactions and some spectacular speculative losses, but it also made money on physical trade. The port of London was the biggest and busiest in the world in the nineteenth century, as Britain supplied the world with manufactured goods and, increasingly, dealt in the commodities produced by its fast-growing empire.

It was the sheer importance of London in the nineteenth century that brought the early international financial, commodity, and capital markets to the City. Today these combine and overlap with the City's UK financial markets, but originally they developed independently of one another.

THE BALTIC

While the internal banking and money market structure was evolving; so too was the City's international position. From the foundations laid by medieval and Tudor traders, new markets were emerging or older ones taking a form that is recognizable today. In insurance and shipping, commodities and finance, London was building a base that was to become virtually unchallengeable long after England ceased to be the world's main source of industrial wealth.

Early informal markets, such as Lloyd's in shipping insurance and the Baltic in shipping, developed into formally constituted markets. Their growth, and indeed the growth of the City's wealth and the scope of the British Empire, was enhanced by the Napoleonic Wars: throughout the eighteenth century Holland was still a more important trading nation, and a more influential financial centre, than England; but in 1796 the Dutch East India Company was dissolved, in 1815 South Africa's Cape Colony was ceded to the British, and in 1819 the highly prestigious Bank of Amsterdam failed.

During the Napoleonic Wars, Britain's overseas trade was maintained and the fiercely protectionist Navigation Acts, which laid down that all trade with Britain should be carried in British ships, gave the Baltic a captive market, and made it the natural place for fixing cargoes. The Navigation Acts were not repealed until 1849. Against this background, the Baltic Mercantile and Shipping Exchange prospered. From its original coffee house haunts, the Baltic moved to its own premises in 1810, and in 1823 the 'Baltic Club' was formed. The Baltic had become – and remains today – the only major shipping market in the world. The finance, insurance and communications facilities of the City are important in maintaining the Baltic's position; but the fact that the Baltic is situated within the Square Mile makes an equally important contribution to the range of services which the City can offer. The Baltic also has a major market in grain futures which developed when grain emerged as a main source of cargo for world shipping.

Lloyd's – to many people the name is synonymous with insurance – grew up in the same manner and at the same time as the Baltic; and the marine underwriting activities of Lloyd's obviously made it complementary to the Baltic's shipping business. Of all the institutions of the City, Lloyd's of London is probably the best known throughout the world for marine insurance and also for undertaking massive non-marine and aviation risks (for example, hurricane insurance) and unusual risks. It draws the line at purely speculative risks which fall into the province of bookmakers rather than insurance, but sometimes the dividing line is a thin one, and it has insured even human features, where the success or notoriety of the possessor of the particular attribute insured has depended upon its continued well-being.

The mystique of Lloyd's rests partly on its phenomenal success, partly on its unique constitution. Membership of Lloyd's is restricted to the very rich: the individual members are responsible for paying out on claims which they have underwritten, and the total security of a Lloyd's policy is dependent on a member's ability to meet his share of any claim. The collapse of the South Sea Bubble was indirectly responsible for the way Lloyd's is structured. Following that first great financial fraud, the government passed an Act, attempting to prevent the worst excesses of financial abuse, which prohibited any company or partnership apart from the Royal Exchange Assurance and the London Assurance Companies from engaging in marine insurance. However, it did not prevent private individuals from so doing on the basis of unlimited liability. Thus the frequenters of Lloyd's Coffee House were able to carry on.

The loose association became more formal, and in 1811 a Trust Deed was drawn up, signed by all the subscribers to Lloyd's. But the Lloyd's as we know it today took rough shape in the Lloyd's Act of Parliament in 1843. This enabled Lloyd's to acquire property, to make binding bye-laws, and set up the Corporation of Lloyd's which takes no part in the business, but sets out stringent conditions governing the way that Lloyd's is run. In practice, Lloyd's is administered by a Committee, elected by the membership. The Committee is responsible for the election of new members and ensuring that the financial stability of members doing business remains adequate. It handles the day-to-day business of the Corporation, including the supervision of the Agency networks and the provision of centralized services.

Subsequent Acts have amended the Lloyd's constitution as conditions have changed, but the underlying mechanism of operation remains the same: approved Lloyd's brokers bring business to the underwriting room and get a syndicate of members – or, in the case of major risks, a number of syndicates – to take up the risk involved. It is a measure of the satisfactory nature of the original concept that it works as well today for jumbo jets and supertankers as it did 300 years ago. The financial requirements of members have increased with inflation, and the number of members of Lloyd's has increased dramatically: today there are over 20,000 underwriting members grouped into more than 400 syndicates, and there are some 270 Lloyd's brokerage syndicates; but the principles of the business are little changed from the days of Edward Lloyd's Coffee House.

INSURANCE

While Lloyd's was busy winning itself a virtual world monopoly in marine insurance, London led in the development of other types of insurance. Not surprisingly, given the City's experience of fire over the centuries, culminating in the 1666 disaster, insurance against fire was the first to gain prominence. After several false starts, the Insurance Office for Houses was founded in 1681 by Nicholas Barbon, and in the next century many other fire offices were to be formed. Perhaps because of its extreme sensitivity to fire, London was a hundred years ahead of other countries in introducing this type of insurance; the lessons it learned were invaluable when it came to exporting insurance expertise.

The same applied to other types of insurance. The Industrial Revolution had enormous social as well as economic implications and led to the introduction of accident and life insurance: in the fast-growing, impersonal, industrial towns there was not the same charitable spirit that might be found in small rural villages in the event of an accident or the death of the breadwinner.

Early life insurance began respectably in a variety of mutual schemes for self-help and, less respectably, as a form of gambling on the longevity of famous people. During the eighteenth century, however, actuarial principles were being worked out that made the commercial provision of life cover viable. Getting there first was one of the two main reasons that Britain's (and therefore the City's) insurance companies were able to win such a dominating position in international general insurance markets, not just in marine insurance. The second reason was the strong international links which British trade forged – particularly with the colonies, but also elsewhere.

A good example of this is provided by the early history of the Phoenix Assurance Company, founded almost exactly a hundred years after Barbon had opened the first fire office. Starting life as the New Fire Office in 1782, the Phoenix was set up by sugar refiners to carry their fire risks at better premiums than could be obtained from general fire offices: sugar refining was a high fire-risk business. Based on its specialist knowledge of the risks involved in sugar refining and on the knowledge of merchants and markets which the British refiners had, Phoenix opened its first overseas office in Nantes just four years after it started trading. The next logical step was to open an office in America, since it was already insuring American-based sugar risks through its London office. Phoenix claims to have been the first UK insurance company to open branches abroad, and many others followed its lead.

Knowledge was just as important as expertise to Lloyd's which built a network of Agents throughout the world, part of whose job it was (and is) to relay the latest intelligence on all shipping matters back to the market. *Lloyd's List*, which has the distinction of being the longest-established daily paper in London, publishes all major shipping news, and has done so since 1734.

'Lloyd's Register of Shipping' is independent of Lloyd's itself, although they share the same origins and have close links; it is the most comprehensive classification of vessels of more than 100 tons in the world. There is no higher recommendation than to be A.1. at Lloyd's.

It is on the base of the nineteenth-century expansion of UK insurance companies abroad that the strength of the City's present-day insurance interests has been built.

Insurance is by far the biggest single element in the City's invisible-earnings contribution to the balance of payments, and British insurance companies do more business abroad (excluding life assurance) than they do in the United Kingdom.

The two biggest companies in the composite insurance sector (composite meaning the company issues general and life policies), Royal Insurance and Commercial Union, have huge worldwide underwriting commitments. Together with the other composites and major broking firms they make London the most competitive insurance market in the world.

PENSION FUNDS

All British government-owned industries offer generous pension benefits to their employees. The money which provides these benefits is channelled into pension funds, whose managers have vast sums of that money to invest.

One of the major problems facing the pensions funds over the next decades is that the amount of money they manage will increase even more dramatically than it has up to now and these funds will gradually become the largest source of investable funds in the country.

They are legally obligated to act in the best interests of their members, which today may mean investing abroad, but they are under increasing political pressure – particularly those in the nationalized industry sector – to support British industry.

The growth of life assurance and, particularly, pension funds in the UK has been quite staggering, and this has had a considerable impact on the City since the vast majority of the money collected finds its way back to the City for long-term investment. At the end of 1980, the total assets of the life assurance companies were around £65 billion, and the investments held by the pension funds are reckoned to total some £62 billion. Servicing these institutions has provided the City with a whole new industry, since the biggest life companies, with the Prudential Assurance at the top of the list, and the biggest pension funds, headed by the Post Office Pension Fund, can measure the new money they have to invest in terms of millions of pounds per week. The banks vie with one another to advise these funds on investment strategy, and the stockbrokers compete for the business of dealing on their behalf. Investment research and investment analysis are essential back-up services in modern City markets, and substantial research teams now figure prominently in the weapons of most major stockbroking firms. This is one of the changes that has affected the development of the London Stock Exchange.

THE STOCK EXCHANGE

It is no exaggeration to say that none of these City markets could have developed in the way they did without the existence of the London stock market. From the seventeenth century, when shares in the merchant venturers' companies changed hands in Jonathan's Coffee House, marketability of securities was an essential link in the chain that eventually bound all the City's finanial and commodity markets together.

In 1773 the dealers moved to 'New Jonathan's', and this became known officially as the Stock Exchange. In 1802 it was formally constituted with 550 subscribers and 100 clerks; with the eclipse of the Amsterdam Bourse, the London Stock Exchange became the undisputed leader in world stock markets, and the first modern stock exchange in embryo. As the Industrial Revolution progressed, other, smaller stock exchanges sprang up around the country to meet local needs, but none ever approached London in size or importance. Until the First World War, the London market was by far the biggest in the world in terms of volume and the capacity to do business.

But a stock market is only efficient if stocks can be freely traded. Buyers will only buy if they are secure in the knowledge that they can sell at any time – whether at a profit or a loss. In today's vast stock exchanges this problem hardly exists: except in highly exceptional circumstances a price can always be struck that will equate desires of the willing buyers and willing sellers. However, this was not always the case; each growing market had to devise its own means of ensuring marketability; London, being first in the field, had to grapple with the problem first. It solved it by the unique method of splitting its members into two categories: brokers, who bought and sold shares on the instruction of clients; and jobbers, who 'made' the market. In London, a broker with a buy or sell order did not have to search for another broker with matching requirements, as happened elsewhere; he could go to one or more of the jobbers who dealt in the shares and be assured that he could deal. The only point at issue was the price at which the bargain was to be struck.

Brokers, unless they deal on their own account, do not take risks; they earn their money on commission. The jobbers act as principals, buying and selling shares in their own right. They make a 'turn' on transactions since at any given moment their buying price is lower than their selling price, but they are also entrepreneurs in the sense that they bear risk. Jobbers have to interpret the likely movement in the market of the shares in which they deal and adjust their buying and selling prices accordingly. If they interpret wrongly, they will find themselves short of stock which is rising in price or long in stock which is falling; in either case they will lose money. If they read the market correctly, however, and lead stocks up or down, rather than following them, they can make substantial profits.

This is another ad-hoc system devised by the City which served the financial community well, and stands the test of time today. The existence of the Stock Exchange allowed the government to fund its ever-increasing National Debt and enabled industry to raise the capital it required, as well as providing for overseas governments and industrial development.

SETBACKS

Scandals and setbacks there were aplenty. The South Sea Bubble scandal of 1720 was only the most spectacular of probably more than 200 highly speculative or outright fraudulent company promotions in the early part of the eighteenth century, and there was similar speculative frenzy in the railway companies during the nineteenth century (and later still in overseas railway stocks). But under the froth there was good, sound investment and, for example, by the middle of the nineteenth century the City had financed the main British rail network, with some 6,000 miles of track.

At the beginning of the twentieth century, Britain stood supreme as a world trading power. It had a huge and profitable Empire; sterling was the world's trading currency, ranking second only to gold, with bills drawn on London regarded as virtually as good as gold. Britain was a net exporter of capital to a massive extent and reaped the reward through trade as well as interest and dividend payments. The City was the financial heart of this great empire of commerce, the undisputed master of the world financial scene.

Two World Wars later, with Britain left victorious but at the expense of crippling overseas debts, the picture has changed in all but one respect. Sterling may no longer be the world's most important or acceptable currency and Britain may be lagging behind as an industrial and trading power; yet the City is still indisputably the world's leading financial centre.

The underlying strength, organization, cohesion and flexibility of the City's markets have remained unchanged. New markets have sprung up, but the City has been quick to adapt to them and actually to strengthen its position by exploiting them. Today's financial markets are vastly more sophisticated than ever before, but coping with these developments has called for adaptation of the City's traditional financial structure, rather than radical change.

The London stock market is now the third biggest in the world, after New York and Tokyo; its daily business averages about £1,000 million. However, the bulk of that is now done on behalf of institutional investors rather than for private investors. With bigger clients and bigger deals, the member firms of the Exchange have to be bigger too. As turnover has increased, the number of firms has fallen, and the provincial exchanges have all merged into a united Stock Exchange, centred in the City.

In 1950 the London market was composed of 364 broking firms and 187 jobbing firms: today the 4,200 members of the London Stock Exchange are concentrated into just seventeen jobbing firms and ninety-four firms of brokers. Because they take risks on their own account, the jobbers need a much bigger capital base than the brokers, and just five major jobbing firms do more than ninety per cent of stock market business. These are Wedd Durlacher, Akroyd and Smithers, Smith Bros, Bisgood Bishop, and Pinchin Denny. Suggestions that this concentration of power inhibits competition were considered to be unfounded by the UK Monopolies and Mergers Commission in 1977 to the extent that the Commission was prepared to approve a merger between two of the big five – although that merger never, in fact, took place.

Rules governing the quotation of and dealings in securities are laid down by the Stock Exchange Council, which is elected by members and is also responsible for punishment in cases where the rules are broken. A compensation fund is maintained to ensure that if any member firm is unable to meet its obligations the cost is borne by Stock Exchange members, so that the general public does not lose money.

During the 1960s there was considerable criticism of some of the tactics employed by companies and their financial advisers in fierce takeover battles. Realizing the validity of the criticism, the Governor of the Bank of England stepped in and, as a result of his initiative, a Takeover Code was worked out and a Takeover Panel set up to administer it. The Panel works closely with the Stock Exchange, and its effectiveness relies solely on the agreement of the financial community to abide by the rules; its only sanction is the power of public censure to undermine the reputation and financial standing of those it criticizes. Having no statutory authority, the Panel carries a massive libel insurance.

This degree of self-regulation, although not uncommon in other City markets, is unheard of in any other major stock market, most of which are controlled by statutory bodies such as the US Securities and Exchange Commission. The London system has two main advantages: first, it works; second, it allows rules to be made or changed swiftly to deal with new situations as they arise, and, unlike the courts, the regulatory bodies are not bound by legal precedent set down by previous decisions. The only concession made to legal control came in 1980 when insider trading – making money on the stock market by using privileged information – was made a criminal offence.

Though primarily a domestic market, the stock market does a considerable amount of overseas business; new rules now allow overseas companies to acquire up to thirty per cent of the shares in any company which is a member of the Exchange, while many members now also have offices in overseas financial centres. London's traditionally international markets have continued to prosper, in spite of attempts at competition from emerging rivals.

COMMODITY MARKETS

As the City's financial markets were developing, so too was its physical trade. It grew throughout the eighteenth century, until London was the biggest and busiest port in the world and the world's main centre for commodity trading. Grain, tea, coffee, cocoa, sugar, spices and many other luxury commodities were shipped into London, either for consumption in the UK or to be re-exported. In return, ships left the Port of London laden with machinery and manufactured goods, the products of the Industrial Revolution.

The commodity markets were concentrated between Mincing Lane and Mark Lane, in an area between the Bank of England and the river, apart from the fur market which was situated further west. The brokers in commodities congregated round the markets where the commodities were auctioned, their job made easier by the fact that the City conveniently provided them with banking, shipping and insurance facilities close at hand. In the early days, some markets had their own buildings (for example, the Wool Exchange), and the East India Company held its sales on its own premises; but others were auctioned – almost inevitably – in coffee houses.

The beginnings of the London Metal Exchange were also in a City coffee house (the Jerusalem), but by the middle of the nineteenth century, the metal traders had moved to the Royal Exchange. Until the opening up of deposits in the new world, England was the world's leading producer of tin, lead and copper. By the time the London Metal Exchange Company formally came into being in the 1870s, Britain's metals production has been overtaken by other countries, and the UK became a net importer. This did not stop the London Metal Exchange from remaining the most important metals market in the world, in the same way that the non-metals commodity markets – later to be merged into the London Commodities Exchange – retained a world importance out of all proportion to Britain's own relatively small (in global terms) commodity requirements.

One reason for this was that the City markets, being long established, were efficient enough to see off potential rivals – and with the Baltic Exchange close to hand, it was not difficult to deal in London, but route the commodities direct from source to end-user without their coming anywhere near the UK. The other reason was that commodity production and the new mining ventures were largely financed by British money, so it was logical to trade through the City which had supplied the capital.

In other commodities, London remains a major world trading centre and, in the case of the London Metal Exchange, *the* major trading centre. The commodity broking network, set up when the City was the physical marketplace for commodities, has remained; these brokers now arrange a substantial proportion of world commodity sales and purchases. Much of London's commodity dealing takes place almost unnoticed, since trading in commodities does not require an actual marketplace.

GOLD

The world's gold market has undergone a considerable change over the last fifteen years. Following the relaxation of restrictions, Zurich made a determined attempt to supplant London as the world's main bullion centre. However, it did not succeed, and twice a day the world price of gold is fixed in London, attended by members of the five London bullion houses, armed with orders for clients from all over the world. The fixing ceremony, held in the fixing room of N.M. Rothschild, is quaint, with each dealer raising or lowering a Union Jack before him, to indicate whether or not he is ready to deal at the suggested price. The biggest gold producer by far in the Western world, South Africa, sells its gold on the London market through the Bank of England, so the City, appropriately, remains the biggest centre for the commodity that still underpins the world's international monetary structure.

A great quantity of Russian gold is reputed to come through the London gold market. The Soviet Union, reputedly the second largest gold producer in the world (although no figures have ever been disclosed) is also acknowledged as being amongst the shrewdest dealers in the metal.

THE EURODOLLAR MARKET

But the most important post-war development, as far as the City is concerned, came in the late 1950s with the emergence of the eurodollar market. US banks were restricted on overseas lending and on the rates of interest they could pay on deposits. As a result of US purchases of European companies, however, there were plenty of dollars in European ownership and, for a variety of reasons, these were much in demand. London was quick to take advantage of US restrictions and captured the lion's share of the market in these dollars. That it was able to do so was owing to a number of factors: London had a banking system that was sufficiently sophisticated and international to deal quickly and efficiently in this new international financial instrument, and a banking system that was governed by flexible guidance rather than by strict legislative control. The Bank of England could easily have prevented London from becoming the eurodollar centre; instead, it actively encouraged the development. Even more important, it maintained its 'open door' policy of welcoming reputable overseas banks, unlike some financial centres which hedge interlopers around with restrictions.

In the 1960s and the early 1970s, banks from all over the world set up in London, with Americans leading the field. Today, there are more American banks in London than there are banks in New York. Older financial centres joined in as well. In 1960 there were only two Swiss banks in London: the long-established Crédit Suisse, and the even older-established Swiss Bank Corporation. By 1980 there were fourteen.

The eurodollar market flourished and grew into the eurocredit market and, with so many foreign banks based in London, it was natural for the City to gain predominance in the foreign exchange market too – again under the benevolent, if watchful, eye of the Bank of England. Foreign-exchange transactions in London are usually made through foreign-exchange brokers, rather than direct between banks.

The overseas banks in London find themselves alternately co-operating and competing with the London clearing banks and the merchant banks, both of which have branched out considerably from their original functions. The clearing banks have expanded significantly overseas – all four now have a major presence in the United States – and have entered the preserves of the merchant banks, either by setting up their own subsidiaries or, in the case of the Midland, buying an existing merchant bank, Samuel Montagu. The commercial banks now offer a whole range of financial services, either directly or through subsidiaries, from leasing to investment advice and euromarket involvement.

The merchant banks have also branched out considerably from their primary activities, using their original assets, individual flair and specialist expertise, to combat the much greater financial asset base of the clearing banks.

THE FUTURES MARKETS

Trading in futures, the right to buy a commodity at its current price at some specified future date, needs a market floor where traders can bid against one another in 'open outcry'. The main importance of futures markets is to allow commodity users to hedge against changes in the price of their raw materials, which might otherwise wipe out the profit they expect to make in their business, and as such is a form of insurance policy. London has three such marketplaces for traditional commodities. The London Metal Exchange operates futures markets in copper, lead, zinc, tin, aluminium and silver, and is the only metals market in the world to trade in all six of these non-ferrous metals. On the floor of the London Commodity Exchange in the Corn Exchange building there are futures in coffee, cocoa, rubber, wool and vegetable oils. In the nearby Baltic there is a grain futures market and a recently opened market in potato futures. It is this range of facilities, backed up by a whole network of ancillary services, that makes London the most comprehensive commodity marketplace in the world.

Lloyd's has just had another Act of Parliament to adapt its structure to present-day needs and to prevent overlapping of underwriting and broking interests; attempts are being made in New York to establish a market that will set up in competition. Lloyd's regards the first as an internal reorganization, although it was prompted by an independent inquiry commissioned by the Committee; it is not much bothered by the second. With a premium income well in excess of £2 billion a year, Lloyd's does three-quarters of its business overseas; as long as its underwriting capacity remains sufficient to cover the ever-increasing size of risks, its reputation and efficiency should ensure its continuing supremacy.

The Baltic Exchange is in a similar position. Three-quarters of the world's open market bulk cargo movement is reckoned to be handled by Baltic members at one stage or another; and the market added aviation chartering to its traditional shipbroking activities with hardly a hitch.

The City has never been slow to introduce new markets, either of its own invention or copies from elsewhere. The investment trust was a City innovation of the late nineteenth century to allow investors to invest in overseas railway stocks with a spread of risk; the introduction of unit trusts was another attempt to popularize equity investment with a good spread of risk. More recently, other more sophisticated markets have been introduced: the stock market now deals in traded options, where options to buy shares in the future can be bought and sold; there is now a gold futures market. It is perhaps a fitting monument to the City's unique character that the latest City market, that in financial futures, has started up in the Royal Exchange, which was first opened for business by Elizabeth I in 1570.

That then is the geography of the financial city. Heading it is the Bank of England, controlling, guiding, encouraging – and sometimes rescuing. In the middle is the wide portfolio of markets, interdependent or complementary, which combine to make the City one immense marketplace: a financial supermarket for the world. Servicing these market are thousands of accountants, solicitors, consultants and agents, all neatly fitting into one square mile. It is impossible to quantify the deals done in total, but in the course of every working hour the City earns more than £1 million in foreign exchange towards the country's balance of payments – and that works out at over £2 per head for everyone who works in the business City, from copytypists to the Governor of the Bank of England.

FINANCIAL CITY

The view from Mansion House towards the heart of the Financial City, showing the Bank of England, the Stock Exchange, the National Westminster Bank Tower, the Royal Exchange and, to the right, Lombard Street. Most of the financial institutions depicted in this volume are within a five-minute walk of this spot.

THE BANK OF ENGLAND

The Chief Gatekeeper and the Assistant Gatekeeper dressed in full livery and carrying the staff of office, in the entrance hall of the Bank of England. In spite of the traditional clothing the role of the gatekeepers is the real one of guarding against unwelcome visitors.

The Bank has been situated at Threadneedle Street since 1734 when its staff numbered one hundred. The present building, extending seven storeys above and three below ground, was completed in 1939 by the architect Sir Herbert Baker, who rebuilt the earlier structure designed by Sir John Soane in 1788.

Affectionately known as 'The Old Lady of Threadneedle Street' based on a famous cartoon by James Gillray which accused the Bank of keeping 'bad company' with the Prime Minister of the day, William Pitt the Younger, the Bank now issues all banknotes for England and Wales. The Scottish and Northern Ireland banks must keep Bank of England notes to back their own issues. Its vaults contain the government's gold and the Bank generally acts as the overseer of all banking activities in the United Kingdom.

The Bank maintains seven branches in England's main provincial cities and a representative office in Scotland. Although its function is that of a reserve or central bank, it does offer banking facilities to some private customers.

Mr John Sangster, Foreign Exchange Division, and Mr David Somerset, Chief Cashier, in an ornate alcove on the Court Room floor. The sixteenth-century Flemish tapestry in the background depicts the meeting between the Queen of Sheba and King Solomon and the sculptured heads depict various early governors.

The signature of the Chief Cashier is probably the best known in the country, since it appears on every banknote issued during his reign. The Foreign Exchange Division is probably unknown to the general public, but the influence it exercises over the daily dealings of the international financial markets is vital to the markets' health.

The Right Hon. Gordon Richardson and Christopher 'Kit' McMahon, Governor and Deputy Governor of the Bank of England in the Court Room of the Bank.

The positions of Governor and Deputy represent the pinnacle of achievement in the financial City. Easily the two most powerful men in the City, their influence is not apparent to the public, but to the financial City their polite request is equivalent to a royal decree. Mr Richardson, a former barrister, has held the post since 1973 and Mr McMahon, an Australian, was appointed in 1980. The two men rule with the aid of the Court, which comprises the four executive directors of the Bank and twelve outside directors drawn from the City, industry and the trade unions. The Court meets every Thursday morning.

THE STOCK EXCHANGE

It is difficult to estimate the exact turnover of an average day's dealings at the Stock Exchange in all securities, but the sum of £1,000 million in buying and selling is a reasonable estimate. That is a mammoth amount of money to be traded every day and is certainly out of proportion to the size of the United Kingdom itself. Only the New York Stock Exchange and Tokyo have a generally larger turnover. However, it must be remembered that the London Exchange comes closest to a truly international exchange where at present 399 foreign companies, hailing from Australia to Zimbabwe, are listed and it offers the largest range and number of listed securities of any stock exchange in the world.

The Exchange is headed by the Chairman, Sir Nicholas Goodison, who meets fortnightly with the Stock Exchange Council, a group of members that governs and regulates exchange dealings. The Chairman's influence extends far beyond the City itself, since his views affect government thinking and policy on many finance- and company-related issues.

Sir Nicholas Goodison, Chairman of the Stock Exchange.

◄ Lord Cromwell, who co-operated enthusiastically with this book, died in a riding accident during publication. As the Senior Government Broker he was one of the most respected figures in the City and the *Financial Times* said of him: 'Since taking over the job eighteen months ago he has introduced more innovations than in the previous two decades'. The editors considered it right to leave the book unchanged because Lord Cromwell symbolized in the finest possible way the office he represented as the agent of the Bank of England.

John Piggot of Bone Fitzgerald, brokers, checking the jobber's board for prices.

David Thorpe, the senior Equity dealing partner of Grieveson, Grant & Co., on the floor of the Exchange.

Anthony 'Tony' Simons, a jobber for Wedd Durlacher at the 'Three Wise Men Pitch'.

Michael Reader, also of Pinchin Denny, consults his dealing book in answer to a query.

Another Wedd Durlacher jobber quoting to a broker from Fielding, Newson Smith & Co.

Michael Rogers, a Pinchin Denny & Co. partner, deals in plantation stocks: rubber, tea, etc.

All representatives of Mullens & Co. are considered government brokers and are recognized by their silk hats.

An overall view of the Exchange, showing jobbers' pitches.

JOBBERS & BROKERS

Brian Peppiatt

Brian Peppiatt may be referred to as a quintessential jobber. The second son of the legendary and longest-serving Chief Cashier of the Bank of England, Sir Kenneth Peppiatt, he was educated at Winchester College and joined Akroyd & Smithers, one of the largest and most successful jobbing firms in the Stock Exchange, at the age of twenty-one. He became a Member of the Stock Exchange in 1956 and a partner of his firm in 1959. In 1981 at the age of forty-seven he became Chairman of Akroyd & Smithers jointly with Timothy Jones.

The lot of the jobber is a difficult one as he buys and sells on his own initiative and uses his own funds. Moreover, buy- and sell-orders are transmitted verbally, later to be completed by each party's office, and therefore the Stock Exchange's motto 'My word is my bond' carries real meaning in terms of each transaction.

Brian Peppiatt is responsible for 162 of his colleagues from Akroyd & Smithers on the floor and he and his colleagues on the gilt-edged pitch frequently deal in £500 million of stock each day, an amount which is significantly exceeded on very busy days.

Brian Peppiatt is married with four children and still lives in his native Buckinghamshire where he maintains a farm, goes salmon-fishing and follows the National Hunt races.

Rowe & Pitman is one of the largest stockbroking firms in the City, and can also claim the largest dealing 'box'. It is from the box that its dealing personnel on the floor keep the firm and its clients in touch with prices and announcements on a minute-by-minute basis during market hours. The firm's dealers' main role is to carry out clients' instructions to buy and sell shares.

A stockbroker with a large international business also has a sophisticated dealing capacity in overseas markets. Rowe & Pitman has offices in San Francisco, Boston, Johannesburg, Tokyo and Hong Kong with whom it is in constant touch. This network of offices enables the firm's clients in Britain and abroad to deal in major world stockmarkets and is an example of the international outlook which has long been one of the strengths of the City.

The Rowe & Pitman dealing box.

THE LONDON DISCOUNT MARKET

The London Discount Market Association comprises twelve discount houses of which Gerrard & National is one of the largest. The Chairman and Deputy Chairman of the Association meet once a week with the Governor or Deputy Governor of the Bank of England to report on conditions in financial markets. The discount houses have an obligation to the Bank of England to tender for the whole of the weekly issue of Treasury Bills. They also supply liquidity to the banking system, and, in their role as bankers to the banks, have deposited with them call money amounting to between £4,000 million and £6,000 million.

Gerrard & National

The Dealing Room at Gerrard & National. The daily turnover here could be as much as £700 million.

Roger Gibbs, Chairman of Gerrard & National, in the courtyard at the Bank of England. The silk hat, which is also worn by the Government Broker, symbolizes the close relationship which exists between the discount houses and the Bank.

Most of the money borrowed by the discount market is secured by 'paper' assets.

LLOYD'S OF LONDON

Gordon Horsley has been a Lloyd's Waiter for twenty-two years. The expression
Waiter dates back to Lloyd's Coffee House

Lloyd's Committee meets under Chairman Sir Peter Green in the Committee Room, designed by Robert Adam.

Lloyd's underwriting members are private individuals who have one thing in common: they are very rich. Lloyd's has more than 20,000 members grouped into over 400 syndicates varying in size from a handful to many hundreds of 'names', as they are called.

On average each member has to have private assets of £100,000 readily available to meet insurance claims for which he assumes unlimited personal liability. It is this type of financial muscle combined with the entrepreneurial skill of professional underwriters acting for the syndicates that enables the Lloyd's market to do business each year worth nearly £3 billion in premiums. All risks insured at Lloyd's are placed by some 270 firms of accredited Lloyd's brokers.

The powerful capital backing of Lloyd's syndicates, estimated to be equivalent to their entire annual premium income, is allied to a chain of security unrivalled among the world's insurers, enabling Lloyd's to assert confidently that valid claims will always be met in full. This security, combined with its underwriting expertise, attracts a wide variety of risks to Lloyd's market, ranging over the years from Marlene Dietrich's million-dollar legs to a pop group concert of the eighties, and from the first aviators to the space explorers of today.

It is impossible to assess the full value of Lloyd's underwriting; however, it can safely be said that it is the most international insurance market and that, despite the massive risks taken almost daily, Lloyd's retains its reputation as the most reliable insurance market anywhere.

Lloyd's is administered by a sixteen-member Management Committee, elected by and from their fellow market members. The Committee meets every Wednesday morning under its Chairman Sir Peter Green and is responsible to the Council of Lloyd's, of which it is a part, an elected body established by the Lloyd's Act 1982, primarily concerned with rule-making and disciplinary matters.

THE BALTIC EXCHANGE

The noticeboard at the Baltic Exchange.

In spite of its imposing building, the Baltic Exchange still manages to retain some of the original coffee house atmosphere in its trading. Looking at the floor of the market, there seems to be no structure to it: people are wandering about with pieces of paper in their hands, others appear to be standing around doing nothing at all.

The appearance is quite misleading: it is estimated that three-quarters of the world's bulk-cargo market passes through the hands of the Baltic's members at some stage.

As well as being the world leader in shipping, there is now a thriving business in aviation chartering. The Baltic's motto, 'Our Word is Our Bond', means exactly that; verbal agreements between Baltic members are totally binding, and this informal manner of dealing makes for maximum efficiency with a minimum amount of fuss.

The floor on any weekday between
11 a.m. and 12 noon.

111

INSURANCE

Commercial Union

The formation of the Commercial Union Fire Assurance Co. was the direct result of the Great Tooley Street fire in 1861. The conflagration, the worst since the Great Fire in 1666, devastated an area of warehouses, wholesale stores and even ships moored on the Thames from St Olave's church to Hays Wharf. As a result the existing insurance companies raised their rates to an exorbitant degree and the City merchants, unable to pay these rates, banded together and started their own co-operative insurance company. The first Chairman, Henry Peek, was a wholesale grocer and his deputy a wine and spirits importer.

Cecil Harris, Chief Executive (centre) meets with his two Executive Directors John Linbourn and Bob Sloan (left) in the magnificent boardroom, overlooking the City.

The company grew rapidly, adding Life coverage in 1862 and Marine Insurance in 1863 and by 1869 the company had appointed its first North American agent in San Francisco. It was there during the San Francisco earthquake in 1906 that CU and British insurance companies in general made their great breakthrough in the USA and established their credibility. By 1869 the company had appointed its first American agent in San Francisco. CU, as the biggest Marine insurer in the most important shipping insurance market in the world, has been involved in most legendary sea disasters, the *Titanic* (registered mail), the *Lusitania* (cargo) and the *Andrea Doria* (general) among many.

Today Commercial Union is one of the two biggest insurance companies in Britain. At last count its premium income from non–life business was in excess of £1,500 million a year, with close to half of that income coming from the US and 79% of the total being earned overseas. This ability to compete successfully in foreign markets is a true indication of the importance of the British insurance market and the respect it commands throughout the world.

Sir Francis Sandilands, the Chairman of CU, is a passionate collector of fine art. The gallery on this executive floor includes a major Francis Bacon, a Graham Sutherland and several other fine paintings and sculptures.

THE LONDON METAL EXCHANGE

The trading ring

Sell one unit

Buy five units

Offer three units

Buy seven units

The London Metal Exchange is the world's leading market for trading in non-ferrous metals. It is the only market in the world to deal in all the seven most important metals: silver, aluminium, copper, lead, zinc, tin and nickel. Deals for cash mean that the metal must be delivered to the buyer the following day, but there is also a futures market. This is conducted on the basis of 'open outcry' in the trading ring of the L.M.E. It is an exciting business: dealers shout their willingness to buy or sell a specific quantity, and other dealers shout their response. There is a lot of hand-waving, and it is a case of first come first served and the devil take the hindmost.

The market is divided into morning and afternoon dealing; each metal is dealt with in five-minute dealing sessions: silver 11.50 – 11.55, aluminium 11.55 – 12 noon, etc., and this makes for a constant frenzy by all those surrounding the Ring.

The frantic buying and selling which takes place during each of the market's five-minute sessions is often transmitted through mysterious hand signals, which overcome the ever-present din of the shouting members. Generally a hand facing towards a person means 'buy' and away from the person 'sell'. Sometimes it is difficult to divine exactly which way the dismembered hands are facing – but these are all market codes, understood by those who have to understand.

NEW FINANCIAL MARKETS

In 1982 two new markets opened their doors in the City of London. The first was the London Gold Futures Market, formed jointly by the London Metal Exchange and the London gold market. The twenty-nine members of the LME and the five gold bullion dealers (three of which were already members of the LME) were instantly joined by seven major investment firms, including the American houses Merrill, Lynch, Pierce, Fenner & Smith (Brokers and Dealers); Dean, Witter, Reynolds Commodities; Shearson American Express; and the Swiss Trade Development Bank; to fill the thirty-eight boxes available.

The market offers dealing facilities in gold by enabling traders to purchase and sell the metal for future delivery based on a margin deposit. The market's location in the City furthermore enables it to bridge the closing of the Far Eastern exchanges with the opening of the American exchanges, a vital link in trading continuity.

The London International Financial Futures Exchange, or LIFFE, as it is already affectionately known in City circles, will permit trading in future contracts in long-dated gilt-edged stocks, eurodollar deposits, and many other financial instruments. LIFFE could have a significant impact on the long-term structure of City institutions since banks, commodity traders, discount houses and stockmarket brokers and jobbers will be able to compete with one another on equal terms in this market. LIFFE is housed in the Royal Exchange, a fact which would have pleased Sir Thomas Gresham, who brought about the building of the Exchange for the reasons of renewal and progress, which LIFFE represents.

THE CLEARING BANKS

National Westminster and Lloyds Bank

All the clearing banks, including Barclays, National Westminster, Lloyds and Midland, have their head offices in the City of London, and they maintain important foreign and domestic banking branches there as well. They are best known, however, for the extensive network of more than 12,000 branches throughout the country.

The huge cash balances generated by these bank branches underpin the entire money market in the City. Lloyds maintains 2,341 branches in the UK.

Lloyds Bank International operates 177 offices in Central and South America, North America and Europe, and is represented in forty-seven others from Bahrain to the USSR. In addition, Lloyds Bank California operates 102 branches throughout that state, and the National Bank of New Zealand operates 195 offices in the southern hemisphere. The international drive continues to expand, and overall assets of Lloyds now stand at £32 billion.

The Annual General Meeting in the Lloyds Bank
Headquarters in Lombard Street. Lord Lloyd, one of the last links
with the family which founded the bank, retired
from the board after twenty-five years.

The World Money Centre

◄ The World Money Centre, National Westminster Bank's foreign exchange nerve-centre, deals in some forty currencies on a worldwide basis, with sterling, dollars and the euromarket currencies constituting the vast bulk of the trade. Fifty dealers, working from a horseshoe-shaped, ultra-modern room where consoles flash, loudspeakers boom out prices and a news-ticker runs along the ceiling, average £3,000 million a day in trading, of which roughly ten percent is traded on behalf of customers. The flags on top of the console denote the currency in which the dealer trades. The fact that Nat West is only one of many City institutions involved in the money market gives some idea of the astronomical sums that change hands in, or through, the City.

Sir Jeremy Morse, Chairman of Lloyds Bank since 1975 is a former director of the Bank of England and a former Chairman of the Committee of Twenty of the International Monetary Fund.

THE MERCHANT BANKS

The term Merchant Bank derives from the fact that merchants traded in bills drawn against the London market, especially in cases where foreign currency was involved. The guarantors of these bills, mostly a group of other merchants, eventually became 'Merchant Banks'.

Morgan Grenfell & Co.

Traditionally the partners in the old merchant banking houses sit together in one room and conduct the firm's business from there. The room is known as the 'Partners' Room'. Also traditionally, no clients are allowed in the room. Here, Christopher Reeves, Chief Executive, shares the room with six of his senior colleagues.

Morgan Grenfell's history dates from 1838 when an American, George Peabody of Boston, Massachusetts set himself up as a merchant and later diversified into banking. His office at 31 Moorgate, George Peabody & Co., was the bank's first. By the time he retired in 1864, he had taken into partnership Junius Spencer Morgan, also a New Englander, who came to live in London and expanded the bank under the name of J.S. Morgan & Co.

The bank's major business then was the financing of the American railroad system and the issue and sale of railroad bonds, but in due course loans were issued on behalf of foreign governments such as China, and a loan to the provisional French government in 1870 of £10 million after the battle of Sedan, was especially daring, but paid off when the loan was repaid at par three years after the Peace of Versailles.

On the death of Junius, his son J. Pierpont Morgan succeeded him and shortly afterward Edward Charles Grenfell, an Englishman, joined the firm. With J.P. Morgan staying mostly in New York, Grenfell took over management of the British bank, a partnership which proved of immense value when the First World War broke out and neither the Bank of England nor H.M. Treasury had the machinery to deal with the huge amount of finance and trade necessary. The Morgan banks on either side of the Atlantic became the natural conduit and although very successful previously the war years dwarfed Morgan's prior growth.

At the outbreak of the war Morgan Grenfell became one of the founding members of the Accepting Houses Committee, an elite committee whose bills are eligible for re-discount by the Bank of England on demand. With the decline of international markets Morgan Grenfell became one of the first merchant banks to advise and finance British industry and that involvement has become the cornerstone of the firm's business.

Today Morgan Grenfell maintains offices in most major countries and its involvement in banking and client services is on a truly global scale. The bank's last consolidated balance sheet stands at £2,130 million.

The foreign exchange desk buys and sells currencies in the spot and forward markets. Its daily trading amounts to hundreds of millions of dollars. The electronic monitors over each man's position are necessary as foreign exchange trading lacks a central market, such as the Stock Exchange. Dealers therefore link their offers through an electronic network. London's position in this type of activity is pre-eminent internationally.

Hambros

A meeting in the panelled boardroom is chaired by
Rupert Hambro, Deputy Chairman, Hambros Bank.

The story of Hambros Bank begins with the odyssey of Calmer Levy who, in 1778, left his native Hamburg to settle in Copenhagen. In keeping with local custom, he adopted his native city's name, which in the official documents read Hambro.

His three sons went on to distinguished careers as merchants, bankers and statesmen in Denmark, Norway and Sweden, and in time the Hambro family became official Court banker in all three countries.

It was Calmer's grandson, Carl Joachim, who, after a visit to Liverpool, realized the importance of the London money market, and in 1839 he moved to England, forming C J Hambro & Son at 70 Old Broad Street with an initial capital of £50,000.

In 1848 the Prussians' attempt to wrest the province of Schleswig-Holstein from the Danes was repelled, but at great cost. Denmark was forced to seek a foreign loan, and Hambros managed a successful bond issue amounting to £800,000. As a result Carl Joachim Hambro was made a hereditary Baron and Hambros was established as an elite City merchant bank.

The Scandinavian link has been strong ever since, and in this century Hambros has continued to finance the governments of Scandinavia, including Finland and Iceland.

Over the years many of the bank's international activities have had a lasting historical significance. In the 1850s Hambros Bank was closely linked with the financing of the unification of Italy. In 1862 Carl Joachim Hambro arranged an informal meeting in London between Prince Wilhelm of Denmark and Greek officials who were seeking a replacement for the unpopular King Otto. This resulted in the eventual elevation of the Danish Prince to the Greek throne. Since that time the bank has acted as fiscal agent to the Greek government.

The bank has been active in silver, setting the price for that metal for a considerable time, and today is active in precious stones, especially diamonds.

In recent times Hambros has been engaged not only in merchant banking and financial services, but its activities have spread into insurance, equipment leasing, gas and oil exploration and even advertising.

Sometimes called the 'Diamond Bank',
Hambros is active in diamond broking and
merchanting.

S.G. Warburg

The story of Sir Siegmund Warburg and his legendary merchant bank, S.G. Warburg, is the great postwar City success story. Mr Warburg, a refugee from Nazi Germany, not only started his bank with little money and even smaller backing from a community which generally resented outsiders, but became one of the best-respected members of the City élite and the very select Accepting Houses Committee.

Today, S.G. Warburg & Co., with close associates in Paris, New York, Frankfurt, Zurich, and Hong Kong, is one of the premier merchant-banking houses in the City. Here Sir Siegmund, third from the right and now in semi-retirement, faces Henry Grunfeld, one of his earliest partners. They are joined by Geoffrey Seligman on his left, the Joint Chairmen of the bank, Lord Roll and David Scholey at the head of the table, and three Managing Directors.

Crédit Suisse First Boston is a merchant bank with a different success story to tell. A postwar partnership between Crédit Suisse, Zurich, and First Boston Corporation of New York, this has been the leading merchant bank in the eurobond market for a number of years, managing $12 billion worth of new issues from its City headquarters in its last audited year. The dealing desk, allowing for seventy-nine positions, is the largest in the City.

Crédit Suisse First Boston Corporation

The Rothschilds

The name of Rothschild conjures up legendary visions of financial derring-do, the battle of Waterloo, Nathan leaning against his pillar at the early Stock Exchange, the name which financed wars and kept kings afloat.

Today the merchant bank of N.M. Rothschild & Sons is still very much a part of the City, although somewhat reduced in its former dominance, and it is still chaired by a Rothschild from the junior branch of the family – Evelyn de Rothschild.

The fixing of the gold price still takes place, a twice daily ritual, at St Swithin's Lane and the result not only sets the price of gold for Britain, but has far-reaching effects throughout the world.

Five firms participate in the London Gold Market fixing – they are Sharpe Pixley & Co., Johnson Matthey Bankers, N.M. Rothschild & Sons, Mocatta & Goldsmid and Samuel Montagu & Co. All are represented here by directors or managing directors.

The Rothschild family's energy is still vital and different branches have gone their separate ways. The Hon. Jacob Rothschild, Nathan's great-great-great-grandson and heir to the head of the English family, Lord Rothschild, who became a scientist, ran the family bank for many years. He now concentrates his efforts on the £200 million publicly quoted RIT, an investment trust which he built to its present strength, and on J. Rothschild & Company Ltd.

THE FOREIGN BANKS

Morgan Guaranty

Morgan Guaranty maintains a catering service for executive dining to which the entire nineteenth floor is given over. The distinct octagonal structure of the Morgan Guaranty Building enhances the spectacular view afforded from every side. Here the Wall Street Room overlooks St Paul's Cathedral.

Morgan Guaranty's foreign trading department is divided into eurodollar, sterling, Middle East and other areas. In the case of oil related transactions, for instance, the major oil companies have direct line connections with each individual dealer. The bank's average daily turnover in eurodollars now exceeds $2 billion and its overall dealing in all currencies $6 billion per day.

A part of the City's strength is its ability to attract foreign banks and financial institutions. At last count over 400 foreign banks were registered here, some as fully fledged UK registered banks and some maintaining representative offices only, but certainly the cream of the world's banking system was doing business in the City.

Morgan Guaranty Trust Company of New York is one of the oldest foreign banks established in the City and the second US bank to open a branch office here in 1897 under the Guaranty Trust name. Today the London office is one of the most active and largest of the bank's international branches, employing well over 1,000 people in the City and at its Stratford operations centre.

The bank, which has long played a major role in the financing of energy resources, has been very active in North Sea oil development. With euromarket syndications centralized in London, the bank has managed or co-managed a total of $54 billion of syndicated loans in 1981 out of its City office.

A district meeting of the General Banking Division. This particular group is involved with companies in the financial field: insurance, banking, broking, investment trusts and pension funds. It is also responsible for companies in the electrical, office equipment, building products, chemicals and pharmaceutical fields. Such specialization gives the bank a decided edge over its competitors in many cases.

Morgan Guaranty's banking division is split into five geographic and industry groups, one of which is headed by Neil Chrisman, Senior Vice President and Group Executive (left), based in New York. He is responsible for the British Isles and Scandinavia as well as commodities and shipping, engineering, mining and construction, petroleum, project finance, real estate and utilities. Here he is in conference in with Albert Vinton Jr, Senior Vice President and Area Manager for the UK, Eire and Scandinavia, and General Manager of the London office. ►

A dealer in the eurodollar market

Saudi International Bank

Saudi International Bank was incorporated in 1975 with the aim of establishing a merchant bank of international scope. Formed at the initiative of the Kingdom of Saudi Arabia, the bank provides wholesale banking services to governments, other financial institutions and major corporations worldwide. Fifty percent owned by the Saudi Arabian Monetary Agency, the bank's other founding shareholders include prominent international financial institutions, led by Morgan Guaranty. Saudi International has become a leading underwriter and manager of loan and securities transactions and plays a large and growing role as a financial intermediary between Saudi Arabia and her trade and business partners. The bank's headquarters are situated in the City with offices in New York and Tokyo and the bank presently has capital funds of £125 million.

View of General Banking Division.

▲ H.E. Sheikh Mohammed Abalkhail, Minister of Finance and National Economy of the Kingdom of Saudi Arabia and Chairman of the Board of Saudi International Bank at the bank's London headquarters with H.E. Sheikh Abdul Aziz Al-Quraishi, Governor of the Saudi Arabian Monetary Agency.

A meeting in the boardroom during the annual general meeting in London includes from left, Guido Hanselmann, General Manager of the Union Bank of Switzerland; the Viscount Sandon, Deputy Chairman of National Westminster Bank; H.E. Sheikh Khalid Algosaibi, formerly Vice Governor of the Saudi Arabian Monetary Agency; H.E. Sheikh Abdul Aziz Al-Quraishi; Lord O'Brien of Lothbury, former Governor of the Bank of England; H.E. Sheikh Mohammed Abalkhail; Walter Page, former Chairman of Morgan Guaranty Trust Company; Dr Mahsoun B. Jalal, Chairman of the OPEC Fund and Eastern Petrochemical Company, plus the bank's Executive Director, Peter de Roos, and its General Manager, Barrett Petty. ▼

Nomura International

Masaaki Kurokawa, the President and Managing Director of Nomura International in the lobby of
Nomura House.

Nomura traders use the computerized communications network to deal with their opposites in Tokyo and their clients worldwide.

Nomura International coordinates the European activities of its parent company Nomura Securities, Japan's largest securities company. The European operation has expanded rapidly since 1964, greatly aided by its philosophy of in-depth research as a prerequisite for sound investments.

The company offers an integrated financial service and trades in all currencies and markets, but particular emphasis is placed on Japanese government and industrial bonds and Yen-related issues. Nomura are also specialists in Gensaki, the simultaneous purchase and re-purchase of Japanese bonds as a short-term investment.

Nomura's intricate satellite-based communications network enables the company to make near instant financial judgements while still fully consulting its worldwide network of companies. The result is a turnover of close to $1.4 billion and an annual growth rate of 21.5%.

Nomura's decision to base its European headquarters in the City mirrors the City's success in attracting the world's major financial institutions.

THE PENSION FUNDS

Hugh Jenkins, Director General of Superannuation Funds for the National Coal Board, looks after funds totalling £2 thousand million and growing at the rate of £300 million a year.

Foreign & Colonial Investment Trust

The Foreign and Colonial Investment Trust, formed in 1868, is the oldest investment trust in the United Kingdom.

The idea of 'spreading the risk' was developed early and the first prospectus stated that the object of the Trust was 'to provide the investor of moderate means with the same advantage as the large capitalist, in diminishing risk in foreign and colonial stocks by spreading the investment over a number of issues'.

The principle remains the same today. The F&C Group, now with assets of £600 million belonging to some 20,000 shareholders has funds invested throughout the free world. The government stocks and railway bonds of the nineteenth century have been replaced by the computer, telecommunications, aerospace and pharmaceutical industry stocks of today and some of the companies which first appeared in portfolios in the 1920s have proved to be the forerunners of Shell, ICI, GEC and other familiar names.

Space-Time Systems is one of the F&C Group's more recent investments. Formed in 1979 with capital from F&C to develop and market computerized box office systems, the company today has installed its system in several UK-based entertainment complexes and is now expanding into North America. Its Barbican installation is here inspected by James Nelson and Michael Hart of F&C.

◄Pension Funds in Britain have assets of about £62 thousand million and these are growing at the rate of about 9% a year. This means that Pension Fund managers have a staggering £6 thousand million a year of new money to invest, most of which finds its way either into property or the stock market.

Pension Funds are second only to the insurance companies in their influence of the market, and with the growth of the index-linked pension it will not be long before collectively they will wield more financial power than anyone else outside of the government.

The biggest funds are those in the nationalized industry sector. Hugh Jenkins, as Director General of Superannuation Funds for the National Coal Board, looks after funds currently totalling £2 thousand million and growing at the rate of some 300 million a year. He has more than £1 million a day to invest.

Although most of this goes into property, the gilt–edged market or equities, around 15% is reserved for direct involvement in industry and commerce. Mr Jenkins's team, for example, have financed several management take–overs. One of a number of success stories in that field is Preformations Group Ltd. It was owned by Plessey until the NCB Pension Funds backed the managers of the company to buy it themselves in 1979. It is now the country's leading manufacturer of industrial magnets, half its turnover is exported and in 1981 it won the Queen's Award to Industry for export achievement.

The NCB Funds also have a stake in Goldcrest Films,   the company behind the Oscar-winning film *Chariots of Fire*. Mr Jenkins is the former Vice Chairman of the National Association of Pension Funds.

VILLAGE CITY

As the presses of Fleet Street spew forth the final editions of Britain's daily national newspapers, the porters are already starting work at Smithfield and Billingsgate, unloading thousands of meat carcasses and over 200 tons of fish each day. At Spitalfields, lorries are arriving with fresh flowers, fruit and vegetables from all over the country and abroad. These are wholesale markets, supplying not only the City but most of the rest of the country with fresh produce. However, the City has its own retail markets too: the Victorian building housing Leadenhall Market contains some seventy shops, selling food and general produce; the street markets, at Leather Lane during the week, and at Petticoat Lane every Sunday morning, sell practically everything to the thousands who flock there.

The City's fame may rest on its supremacy in multi-billion pound international finance deals, but the Square Mile is a living City in its own right. After a long period of decline, its residential population is growing again. It has the biggest arts and conference centre in Europe; it has its own university, schools, parks and gardens – and its own, very special, village atmosphere.

It is no easy matter to retain a clearly defined sense of community when almost all the daytime population leaves every evening, but the City has achieved just that and has produced a remarkable sense of community involvement and civic pride.

The railways and the London underground train system brought about the demise of the original residential City. The population moved out to the suburbs, and houses were converted into, or made way for, offices. Outside working hours, the City was left to the caretakers and the cats.

By the beginning of the Second World War, there were probably only a couple of thousand people living in the City, but on the night of 29 December 1940 the Luftwaffe devastated seventy acres to the north of St Paul's Cathedral, paving or, rather, clearing the way for the most imaginative inner-city reconstruction project ever seen in Britain. It was Duncan Sandys (now Lord Duncan-Sandys) who, as Minister of Housing and Local Government in 1955, suggested a comprehensive and self-contained development of the site, to include shops, schools, arts and cultural facilities, but with the overall accent heavily on residential accommodation.

The City responded, and the Barbican concept was born. The means by which that concept became reality is a typical City story. It took a great deal longer than it should have done to come to fruition, partly because of external factors beyond the City's control, such as strikes, and partly because the concept itself kept changing in points of detail as different pressure-groups strove to impose their version of perfection on the blueprint. Consequently, the project has always been controversial – it has also cost a great deal more than was originally intended. Even the project's most ardent supporters would agree that it is not an architectural masterpiece, but some of the most voluble critics of the scheme now admit privately that in the long term it will prove to be a success story.

The Barbican site now covers some forty acres of the City; it houses between 4,000 and 5,000 residents, raising the City's live-in population to around 7,000. Its 2,114 flats and maisonettes, which can actually house up to 6,500 people, are organized in terraces and three giant tower blocks – at 420 feet high, the Shakespeare Tower is the tallest residential building in the country and merits a mention in the *Guinness Book of Records.*

The Barbican is modelled on the podium principle which segregates pedestrian traffic from all vehicles and is just part of a much more ambitious project to create a pedestrian walkway system, that will eventually allow residents, workers and tourists to walk from one end of the City to the other without having to cross a single traffic-laden street.

The plans for the residential Barbican were finally given the go-ahead in 1959 but, because of delays, its construction was not completed until 1975. By that time the original estimated cost of £17 million had escalated to an actual cost of £50 million. However, although the Barbican Estate operates at a revenue loss of £4 million a year – all met from the rates, since there is no central government subsidy – it is now estimated that the current value of the buildings is around £140 million.

One feature of the Barbican development gives a high density of population coupled with a high percentage of open space: the tower blocks may not look pretty, but they can house a lot of people and, as a result, more than half the Barbican's forty acres are devoted to open space and eight acres to landscaped gardens, including a lake. The historic church of St Giles Cripplegate has been retained, and the planners have allowed fragments of the original Roman wall to remain. The effects of this are often quite striking, as when one turns a corner and suddenly finds the City's oldest standing side by side with the new.

Besides the Barbican development, there are well over a hundred open spaces maintained by the Corporation within the Square Mile – some tiny, some the size of a small park – and each in its own way adds colour and elegance to relieve the monotony of faceless office buildings. Indeed, the City's efforts in this direction stretch far beyond its own boundaries. In the last century it obtained parliamentary approval to purchase land outside the City limits for the benefit of all Londoners. Few people are aware that two famous beauty spots, Epping Forest and Burnham Beeches, are owned and maintained by the City Corporation . . . and these are only the best known; the City owns another half-dozen as well.

Within the Square Mile, the Corporation seeks active support from private enterprise in striving to make the place look more attractive: the Gardeners Company offers prizes for the best displays of windowboxes and gardens, and firms engage in fierce competition with each other to win these awards.

But the Barbican remains the City's most modern showpiece; the focal point of the whole of the Barbican is the Barbican Centre. Completed much later than the residential part of the development – it was opened by Her Majesty the Queen on 3 March 1982 – it provides the City with a cultural and educational centre that will form the foundation of the living City for the future. It has provided a permanent home for the Royal

Shakespeare Company and the London Symphony Orchestra; for the Guildhall School of Music and Drama; and for the London School for Girls – one of three schools owned and administered by the City Corporation. Now officially entitled the 'Barbican Centre for Arts and Conferences', its facilities extend far beyond those already mentioned. It incorporates three cinemas, exhibition halls, conference facilities, restaurants and bars and a top-class library.

The growing cost of the Barbican Centre complex nearly brought about the abandonment of the whole scheme. If the residential side was controversial, the debate on the Barbican Centre was traumatic: the final cost has not yet been assessed, but is likely to prove to be in excess of £160 million, against an original estimate of £18 million.

Ranking alongside others of hundreds of years ago, 15 April 1971 will be seen as an important date in the City's history: upon that day the Court of Common Council met to decide whether the Barbican Centre should go ahead. That Common Council meeting has the distinction of being the longest in the 800 years of the Court's history: it lasted nearly five hours. Councillors, already concerned about the way the costs of the residential Barbican were spiralling, expressed reluctance to commit themselves to what appeared an even more grandiose and expensive project. Eventually they gave grudging consent, and history will probably thank its lucky stars they did. The centre has had its problems and its critics, but it has brought a new dimension to City life. The Barbican is now alive in the evening as well as during the day: top-class performers from all branches of the arts attract thousands to the theatre and the concert hall, and the night-time City is no longer the province of cats and caretakers alone.

Important as the Barbican is to modern-day City life, it would be a mistake, however, for it to overshadow other aspects of the living City. Theatres and restaurants, pubs and clubs, newspapers and churches, hospitals and horses, police and politicians, all contribute to the vitality of the Square Mile which complements its historical and financial importance.

The City's other theatre, which occupies a special niche in the affections of the City is the Mermaid. It was in the late 1950s that the Corporation granted 'Bernard Miles and other poor players of London' a lease of Puddle Dock opposite *The Times* building in Printing House Square. Bernard Miles is now Lord Miles in recognition of his services to the theatrical profession, but the Mermaid itself has often had to exist on a shoestring budget. Even so it has initiated many imaginative productions, a number of which have gone on to be West End hits.

A stone's throw away from the Barbican, in a street that looks to be full of derelict warehouses, Whitbread's brewers stable their shire horses; Pomp and Circumstance, Pride and Prejudice and half a dozen more, each weighing about a ton, are fed four times a day and take a lot of training and looking after. However, they are still regarded as an economic proposition for delivering the company's beers to its City pubs, as well as a good advertisement. They are named in pairs, and normally work in pairs; once a year, six of them combine to pull the Lord Mayor's State Coach. They are also lent by the company for other state occasions.

Whitbread's is not the only stable in the City: the City Police also have one for their mounted branch. The City police force is the Corporation's pride and joy, because it is the only police force in the country that is not directly under the control of the Home Secretary. The right to appoint the Commissioner rests with the Court of Common

Council, and is subject only to the authority of the sovereign. In the case of other local authorities, half the cost of the police force is met by the Treasury; in the case of the City of London, the Treasury only supplies a third of the cost. City policemen are taller than other policemen: the minimum height requirement to join the police force nationally is 5 feet 8 inches; the City Police requirement is 5 feet 11 inches – and traditionally most of them top six feet, even before they don their unusual, Roman-style helmets which make them look taller still.

Officially, the City Police have existed since an Act of Parliament of 1839, a few years after Sir Robert Peel created a statutory police force in this country; but the City Police contend that the 'Peeler Act' modelled other forces on a system already in operation within the City. The City force employs nearly 900 police officers and close to 400 ancillary civilian staff. Given that they cover just one square mile, that is a very high concentration compared with other forces; but the City Police have several unusual roles to play, foremost among which is the unusually high number of ceremonial duties that have to be performed: St Paul's, Guildhall and the Mansion House are only three of the important ceremonial locations on their 'patch' and, as one senior police officer remarked, 'Royalty seems to pop in and out almost every other day.'

A second problem is that the City is a prime target for theft – and almost always by people from other areas. The third explanation requires no further expansion: the City Police maintain a large Fraud Squad.

The City Police are popular within the Square Mile and enjoy their somewhat unusual status. There is a high degree of *esprit de corps* and no shortage of potential recruits; unlike some other forces, they never have to advertise.

But if there is a high proportion of City bobbies in relation to the amount of ground they have to cover, there is an even higher concentration of churches. There are over forty in the Square Mile, and although almost half of them hold regular Sunday services, they have had to come to terms with the fact that the majority of their potential congregations are nine-to-five, Monday-to-Friday commuters. Services are held during the week, early in the morning or at lunchtime; but most City churches try to do a good deal more to cater for their unique audience: on almost every day of the year there will be music recitals, talks or discussions at some of the City's churches, and speakers are drawn from the widest possible range of specialities.

The nature of the City's business and the migrancy of its population make for strange eating and shopping habits. Being a retailer in the City is not an easy task: rents and rates are high, there is virtually no Saturday trade outside the tourist season, and on weekdays most City shopping is done either between noon and three in the afternoon or in quick dashes during coffee breaks. Such restrictions do not necessarily apply to the City's business élite, and there are still some splendid up-market emporia around. Asprey's, Mappin and Webb and Dunhill all have shops in the City, there are still excellent gunsmiths, and tailors run businesses where quality and service are a prime consideration – at a price. In Cheapside, still the City's main shopping street, there are none of the giant supermarkets that are a feature of high streets in other parts of London. As the City's financial contribution to the Greater London Council has risen dramatically, it has been forced to push rates higher still, and this has made it increasingly difficult for small retailers to survive. This is a matter for concern to the Corporation, which has frequent discussions with representatives of retailing groups. The trend is increasingly towards self-service and the use of modern equipment to reduce retailers' overheads. A traditional cobbler could not hope to stay in business in the City, but a modern, fast-service heel bar can still make money.

The eating habits of the City deserve a book to themselves because many of them are built round the unique tradition of the 'city lunch'. Nowhere else in the world do so many business telephone-calls end with the phrase 'let's fix up some lunch', and nowhere else in the world can so much business be done over oysters and lobster, or steak and kidney pie with two veg . . . or even a glass of wine and a sandwich. It is a very good thing that Portugal is England's oldest ally, for surely nowhere else is so much port consumed by so few in such a small area and in such a short space of time!

The City offers a tremendous variety of restaurants, with the emphasis on traditional English fare; but French, Italian, Chinese, Japanese and many other cuisines are also available. The types of eating place vary enormously too. It would be fair to say that the majority of the City's eating houses would not greatly interest Egon Ronay, but there are some top-class restaurants, such as Le Poulbot in Cheapside and Ashleys in Copthall Avenue. Also, as befits the City's traditional links with Billingsgate, there are some excellent fish restaurants: well-known examples include Wheelers and Sweetings.

But the City restaurateurs are interested in the culinary desires of their clientèle far more than in the view of Mr Ronay and, fish apart, that tends towards steaks, roast beef and steak and kidney pie with two veg, whether the surroundings be the historic George and Vulture, famed for its links with Dickens, or the more mundane surroundings of the Throgmorton Restaurant, opposite the Stock Exchange.

It is a strange business, running restaurants, wine bars or pubs in the City. Few restaurants open at all in the evening, and many of the pubs and wine bars close early – except around Fleet Street, of course. Their entire trade is therefore crammed into a hectic three hours between noon and three o'clock, and for most of them 'hectic' is the right word. The best guarantee of security for those transacting business over the lunch table is the general cacophony of sound rather than the distance between tables.

In the restaurants and wine bars frequented by the Stock Exchange broking fraternity, one feature used to be 'blue buttons', junior employees of Stock Exchange firms allowed on to the trading floor but not allowed to deal, rushing in and out with important messages for lunching partners. Today, technology has taken over, and messengers have been replaced by electronic bleepers giving the summons to the nearest telephone, or hotfoot back to the Stock Exchange floor.

Wine bars are becoming an increasingly popular feature of the City scene. Traditional wine bars, such as the Jamaica Inn – handily placed next door to the George and Vulture – and less ancient but well-established names such as Coates Brothers, Bow Wine Vaults, and Balls Brothers, are being joined by newcomers. The City is full of unusual restaurants and restaurants with unusual histories. There is the *Princess Elizabeth*; a retired paddle-steamer moored just west of London Bridge; originally a ferry, now offering bar and restaurant facilities, the *Princess Elizabeth* has the unusual distinction of having won a battle honour for her part in the evacuation of Dunkirk.

City pubs come in as many shapes and sizes as city restaurants. Ye Olde Watling, for example, dates back to 1666 and stands in Watling Street, which is at the site of the start of the original Roman Watling Street. Perhaps the best-known City pub – certainly to the tourist population – is the Cheshire Cheese. The current building was built in 1667 after the Fire and has the distinction of having been the meeting place of Dr Johnson and his cronies, situated in Fleet Street.

Fleet Street is another unique aspect of the City of London. It is to newcomers what Lombard Street is to banking: the most famous name in the world.

There is absolutely no good commercial reason why Britain's national newspapers and the London offices of many important regional papers should be concentrated in this historic street. Indeed, as giant articulated lorries with tons of newsprint block the flow of City traffic and try to negotiate tiny alleyways to deliver their cargoes to the presses that will print tomorrow's papers, there seem to be good reasons why the newspaper world should *not* be situated there. Again, one has to look a long way back into history to discover the reason. Caxton introduced the printing press to England in 1476, but it was some years later when his pupil, appropriately named Wynkyn de Worde, set up, first in Fleet Street and then a little further east in St Paul's Churchyard. The fact that great national newspapers such as the *Daily Express* and the *Daily Telegraph*, and worldwide news agencies such as Reuters and Associated Press, find themselves located within the City boundaries can be traced back to the decision of a fifteenth-century printer.

Some great papers have never been printed in Fleet Street itself. The oldest national daily paper, *The Times*, used to be a stone's throw away south of 'the Street', in Printing House Square; and the *Financial Times* has always been a little nearer the centre of the financial City, further east of Fleet Street, but still close. Fleet Street still retains its own unique and contradictory atmosphere. The most famous watering-hole of legendary hard-drinking journalists, El Vino's, is exactly opposite the offices of the *Methodist Recorder*.

The relations between the City and its irrepressible child, the newspaper industry, are surprisingly cordial. The British press has an enviable worldwide reputation for the accuracy and responsibility of its reporting; and this accords well with the City's own image. Relations between the financial City and the financial reporters are even more interesting. The two professions live in close proximity to each other, to the extent that some national papers, such as the *Daily Telegraph* and its sister paper, the *Sunday Telegraph*, maintain separate City offices closer to the heart of the financial City than the parent offices in Fleet Street.

The *Financial Times* occupies a special place in the City's affections because, in spite of the increasing emphasis on its international coverage, the *Financial Times* is still regarded as the financial City's own 'trade paper'. Its library is largely used by City companies on a subscription basis, as it is regarded as just about the best source of business information there is; the Fraud Squad also uses it for background information 'in the course of its inquiries'.

But the best City journalists are those who abide by the City's own rules: personal contact and absolute trust. Editors, City editors and other leading journalists are often privy to information which, in theory, they should not have. Off-the-record conversations and non-attributable briefings allow journalists to avoid mistakes without disclosing confidential information. Woe betide the journalist who makes improper use of such information or, for that matter, anyone who uses the system to mislead the press. Such occasions are, however, rare, and this tradition, like so many other City traditions, succeeds because it works.

There are many other fascinating faces to the City. St Bartholomew's Hospital, for example, now ranks as one of London's top teaching hospitals, some 900 years after its initial foundations were laid by the monk Rahere. St Paul's Cathedral is not only a monument to Sir Christopher Wren, it is the location for many major ceremonial occasions, the most famous in recent years being the wedding between His Royal Highness, Prince Charles, and Lady Diana Spencer; the Cathedral also runs one of the most famous choir schools in the country.

Perhaps the most surprising omission from a list of notable features of the City is that it does not house the headquarters of Britain's major industrial companies. One obvious reason is lack of space – and anyway there are two exceptions that prove that particular rule. One is British Petroleum, comfortably Britain's biggest trading company, and ranking with the other great multinational companies in the world. The other is Unilever, with its headquarters site by Blackfriars Bridge; it is the biggest company in the world that deals in branded and packaged consumer goods.

Unilever as a company is not too well-known around the world to the people who use its products, but its product brand-names are known to literally hundreds of millions of people around the world. The BP name on the other hand is connected worldwide with just one product: oil. In fact the group also has major interests in natural gas, chemicals, and many other oil and chemical-based products.

The BP building, Britannic House was built in 1967 and, at 400 feet high and with thirty-five floors, was one of the first skyscraper buildings on the modern City skyline. From it BP runs 1,900 companies around the world, employing 153,000 people. To emphasize the City's traditional links between old and new, one of the world's highest technology companies has a special relationship with the Tallow Chandlers Company – whose records go back to at least 1303.

VILLAGE CITY

The City is probably the most floral area in all of Greater
London. There are dozens of pocket-sized
parks tucked away between steel and glass edifices and on a
sunny day City professionals can be seen lunching and enjoying
the sun in the pleasant atmosphere of these parks.

The City institutions keep an army of gardeners solvent, since
most houses display window boxes which are kept in bloom
throughout the year with an everchanging variety of flowers.
Some, like the Bank of England, employ their own gardener and
maintain their own garden centre.

Every working day more than 300,000 people stream into the City of London and a large proportion of ►
them arrive from the suburbs on British Rail. The Gothic style Liverpool Street Station, (over) named after
Lord Liverpool, was completed in 1875.

THE CITY MARKETS

Smithfield Market

The City markets are an active reminder of the early City. To see them in operation in the early hours of the morning in the middle of this place of commerce and high finance is an incongruous sight.

Smithfield, now the country's primary wholesale meat market, was established long before the signing of the Magna Carta in 1215. Looking down the great centre hall covered by an Italianate dome of iron and glass, with row upon row of carcasses displayed in meticulously clean surroundings, is a tourists' delight.

Billingsgate fish market, situated on the river Thames and only a few yards away from Fishmongers' Hall, also can trace its beginnings to Shakespearean times. Recently the market moved down river to the regret of most of the merchants established there for hundreds of years, but the new market, though outside of City limits is still managed by the City Corporation. After an archaeological dig for a Roman market, reputed to lie under the site, is completed, an office building is planned here which however will incorporate the present structure.

Billingsgate Market

153

Leadenhall market with its Galleria style ornate glass-domed ceiling is well worth a visit for its architecture alone. Situated across the street from Lloyd's, it is a wonderful, old-fashioned retail market offering all things edible from meats to fruits and vegetables. Spitalsfield, not pictured here, the wholesale flower and fruit market, is also located in the City.

Leadenhall Market

The City is in a constant state of renewal. Although aware and very protective of its architectural heritage, the destruction caused by the 1941 German Blitz laid waste to large sections of the City and the rebuilding created the present high-rise skyline.

It seems almost daily, tall buildings are replaced by taller ones, for after money space is the City's most valuable commodity.

High office buildings crowd one of Christopher Wren's seventeenth-century churches.

CITY OF LONDON POLICE

The City has had its own police force since the eighteenth century, but the force was formally recognized as separate from the Metropolitan Police by Act of Parliament in 1839. The City police wear distinctly different uniforms and helmets, which is one sign of their independence. They are also the only police force in the country not under the direct control of the Home Secretary.

Today the force averages about 800 men and women and its Commissioners are appointed by the Court of Common Council, subject only to the authority of the Sovereign. Because of the City's many functions officers are often called on for ceremonial duties as well as normal police work.

The City Police Communication Centre is connected to Scotland Yard's information and traffic control centres and will shortly be connected to the Metropolitan Police Command and Control System.

Constable Raymond Hayter, forty-eight years old, joined the City Police in April 1963 after a stint in the Royal Air Force. Married, with two daughters and a teenage son, he serves as a guide at the City of London Police Museum aside from his regular foot-patrol duties.

SCHOOLS

City of London School for Girls

Student in chemistry analysis class.

Many schools on every educational and craft level have been based on the centuries of public consciousness, civic responsibility and generosity of the City livery companies and the City Corporation itself. The City of London School for Girls is one of the oldest and the best.

Founded in 1894 by the Corporation, it remained until 1969, on a site in Carmelite Street. The school now occupies a fine building, complete with superbly equipped classrooms, a gymnasium, a swimming pool and a playing field, which the Corporation provided in the heart of the Barbican complex.

About 640 girls, all day students, come from a thirty-mile radius of the City, attracted by the high standards set by the school in both the sciences and the arts. 'We send many of our girls on to medical or veterinary schools,' says Miss Mackie, headmistress since 1972 'but many girls follow courses in law, or concentrate on languages and music, as our music programme is comprehensive. We also provide courses in five languages, including Latin and Greek.'

Students are eligible from the age of seven until nineteen.

Art class.

Guildhall School of Music and Drama

Ernest Berk, here teaching a movement class to drama students, has been a member of the Guildhall teaching staff for over ten years and is now head of department.

The Guildhall School of Music opened its doors in 1880 in a disused warehouse near Guildhall with sixty-two students. Today, having added drama classes to its curriculum and enlarged its name, the school is housed in the Barbican and caters to 650 full-time students, over 600 part-time students and 200 youngsters under seventeen who attend special Saturday classes. More than 500 attend music classes.

The school teaches almost every solo instrument plus ensemble playing and the drama department offers all the theatre arts from acting and directing to set design.

All the teachers are working professionals who take on one or more classes a term and most students go on to either professional or teaching careers.

The fine reputation of the Guildhall School gives great pride to the City Corporation, whose Music Committee administers and finances the school on behalf of the Court of Common Council. Many private City Corporations contribute to the school's Scholarship Fund.

Ula Kantrovitch, a former Gold Medallist herself, has been teaching cello classes at the Guildhall School for four years. She feels that the school offers the highest standards and integrity and she loves working with talented students such as Wendy Sullivan of Goldsmith College. She concentrates on style, intonation and tone quality and here the Brahms *E Minor Sonata for Cello and Piano* is rehearsed. Mrs Kantrovitch still freelances for, among others, the BBC Symphony and the Halle as well as performing in chamber music recitals.

BRITISH PETROLEUM

Peter Walters, Chairman, stands before the portrait of the company's first Chairman
William Knox D'Arcy, the legendary figure who started the City connection.

It may seem ironical that in the age of the great corporations the City harbours only two large manufacturing enterprises within its borders, Unilever and British Petroleum. These corporations deal principally in commodities far removed from the early manufacturing guilds such as the Coach and Harness Makers, the Cutlers or the Gun Makers.

BP, as it is known, is Britain's largest company, and although its legendary nose for finding oil (it has discovered fifteen of the world's thirty largest fields currently in production outside the Soviet bloc) has produced a colossus comprising 1,900 companies which give employment to more than 150,000 people in virtually every country in the world, BP has always had its headquarters in the City.

When William Knox D'Arcy discovered the first known Middle Eastern oil source at 4 a.m. on May 26 1908 at Masjid-i-Sulaiman in Persia, after seven frustrating years of failure which brought him close to bankruptcy, he formed the Anglo-Persian Oil Company which rented offices on the second floor of Winchester House.

The company soon moved on to Gresham House, thence to Britannic House in Great Winchester Street and finally the eminent architect Edwin Lutyens was hired to design the second Britannic House in Finsbury Circus. In the Renaissance style, it is still one of the most graceful buildings in the City.

Today BP conducts its business from one of the first tall buildings that have transformed the City skyline, a stone's throw away from the Barbican Centre.

BP's intimate involvement with the City has grown over the years. It raises the massive sums of money needed for oil exploration through City institutions. It is very active in the City's life as well, contributing scholarships to such diverse institutions as the Guildhall School of Music and Drama and the City of London Schools for Boys and Girls; contributing towards a Chair at City University; helping support the Mermaid Theatre, the City of London Festival and the City of London Sinfonia Orchestra. Many of its charitable contributions are City-oriented.

BP Shipping are one of Europe's largest shipowners and operators. Here Ian Telfar, BP's Chief Naval Architect, inspects plans of a new liquid natural gas carrier with two of his staff.

A geologist and a geophysicist of BP Exploration Ltd. evaluate oil prospects in the South China Sea. The Exploration Map Library which overlooks the City, is kept locked and under surveillance at all times.

British Petroleum requires large amounts of capital to finance its immense and varied oil operations, in particular the development of new oil fields, and its other natural resources activities.

Robin Adam, Deputy Chairman with responsibility for Finance works closely with merchant bankers Lazard Brothers to raise the necessary funds.

Here he meets in conference with Ian Fraser and Verner Wylie, Chairman and Deputy of Lazard Brothers. In 1981 the Lazard team as lead underwriter, together with the Morgan Grenfell and J. Henry Schroeder Wagg merchant banks, raised £624 million in an issue which is considered to be the largest amount of money ever raised on either side of the Atlantic in new equity capital.

ACCOUNTANTS

The City is served by an army of lawyers, accountants and other professional men and women and many of the country's most prestigious firms are indeed located in the City.

Sir Kenneth Cork, a former Lord Mayor, is the Senior Partner of a highly respected firm of chartered accountants, which has practised within the City for many decades.

Sir Kenneth has long been in the forefront of the movement to encourage closer links between the traditional City and the modern business and professional City.

THE MEDIA

Geoffrey Owen, Editor and Alan Hare, Chairman of the Board of
the *Financial Times*.

The United Kingdom is one of the few countries where newspapers are produced on a nationwide level. The *New York Times* or the *Frankfurter Allgemeine* serve their specific cities, but *The Times* or the *Daily Telegraph* are national newspapers.

Most of these national papers maintain their offices, editorial staffs and printing plants on or near Fleet Street, the street of ink, and a large number of provincial papers also maintain a presence, for Fleet Street is the hub of newspaper publishing in Britain.

Alone among the City institutions the papers' staffs work late into the night and the famous pubs lining the street, such as El Vino, are thronged at lunch and in the evening with journalists discussing scoops and deadlines, stories past and stories yet to come. Although the street boasts many well-known and well-paid women journalists, this is very much a man's world, and several unsuccessful law suits have been brought against El Vino for a woman's right to lean against the bar.

The distinctively pink *Financial Times*, published in the City at Bracken House, near St Paul's Cathedral, is regarded as essential reading by every City-oriented businessman. The *FT*'s coverage of international business news is exhaustive and its reputation for accurate and authoritative reporting places it among the major newspapers of the world.

The *Financial Times* is read on a global scale. All of Europe and the USA read their *FT* on the day of publication, while a hand-delivery service to thirty-five major cities, including Tokyo, Hong Kong and Mexico City, links the rest of the world.

The *Daily Telegraph* is a true Fleet Street paper, and as with the other daily and Sunday papers the City Editor oversees coverage of City news, including the laying bare of those too greedy or those not quite fit to be members of the club.

Andreas Whittam Smith, City Editor of the *Daily Telegraph* at the Gold Futures Exchange with Keith Smith, its Chairman.

Colour Sergeant Edward White

Much of the confidential messenger and administration work in the City is performed by the Corps of Commissionaires. These thoroughly vetted veterans in their distinctive blue uniforms, some sporting their military decorations, are seen all over the City delivering confidential documents, guiding visitors around the various premises and acting as doormen/guards.

Colour Sergeant Edward White, a much decorated veteran of the Second World War, has been a fixture at Quilter Hilton Goodison & Co. since 1950, where he acts as receptionist and confidential messenger.

Other vital support personnel – in addition to secretarial staff – include large numbers of caterers, security specialists and chauffeurs.

Guildhall staff members

SHOPPING

The City's village atmosphere for a long time retained the High Street appearance of small nondescript stores. But over the years many of the West End luxury stores and boutiques have opened City branches here, making a trip outside City boundaries unnecessary. Stores such as Asprey's, Mappin & Webb and Dunhill's are established here and many fine tailoring and haberdashery outfits, especially those specializing in fitted uniforms, are tucked away in small corners.

John Asprey, Chairman of Asprey's of Bond Street, in the City branch, which opened for business in 1959.

Afred Dunhill's City branch opened in 1982.

A shop selling rare books.

DINING

Most major and many of the smaller City institutions employ catering staffs for both executive and employee dining facilities. Some of these 'company' restaurants as those at the Bank, the Stock Exchange, Lloyd's of London, Lloyds Bank, to name only a few, can be counted as among the best in the City and certainly the most spacious and elegant.

Furthermore the City offers public dining facilities which range from hundreds of small cafes to a restaurant featuring belly dancing as one of the attractions. Many executives eat lunch at their desk, since some international market openings such as New York interfere with a leisurely lunch hour.

Still, food is taken seriously in the City and a number of fine restaurants are established here. A typical lunch might start with a pint at the Jamaica Inn and end with a step across the small alley to the George and Vulture, one of the City's favourites, specializing in hearty English fare, or a private dining room might be hired at the Bow Wine Vaults, where fine wines and spirits are also sold separately.

Le Poulbot, run by Michel and Albert Roux, the celebrated chefs who also run London's renowned two star restaurant Le Gavroche, is considered by many to be the best in the City.

Albert and Michel Roux in front of the bar at Le Poulbot, one of their two City restaurants.

The London Marathon, which winds its way through the City is seized on by many normally sedentary and desk–bound City business men, as an opportunity to raise funds for charity. One well–established competitor finished the distance in four hours and fifty–eight minutes, perhaps not an Olympic feat, but as a result he was able to donate a cancer scanner to one of London's specialized hospitals. This sense of public consciousness and civic responsibility is very much a part of the City's spirit.

Whitbread's Brewery has been an integral part of City life ever since Samuel Whitbread established the company here in 1742. The drays pulled by the magnificent white shire horses are a common sight as they make their stately and leisurely progress through the City streets delivering barrels to the brewery's City pubs. These horses also have the singular honour of pulling the Lord Mayor's coach each year during the Lord Mayor's Show. Whitbread's maintains its stables in the Barbican area.

THE MUSEUM OF LONDON

The Museum of London, housed in a circular building at the edge of the Barbican, houses the most complete collection of art and artefacts concerning the City's historic past. Some 8,000 items are on display, ranging from Roman stone fragments and a re-created Roman kitchen area to medieval sculptures and later pieces in gold and silver, jewellery and paintings of the time.

The museum's rooms are divided into time periods, so that a stroll from entry to exit tells the story of the City and London as a whole through the ages. Many of the exhibits are a part of integrated displays which re-create the manner in which these items were used.

Aside from the regular exhibit several special shows are mounted. This one deals with the art of London silversmithing from 1680 to 1780 and some of the City's livery companies loaned their treasures for display.

THE MERMAID THEATRE

Lord and Lady Miles.

It was in the 1950s that the City Corporation chartered the lease of premises of Puddle Dock near Blackfriars, an area devastated by the Second World War to 'Bernard Miles and other poor players of London' and the Mermaid Theatre was born. So important was the Mermaid regarded by the City that the bells of St Paul's Cathedral rang in the opening show, *Lock Up Your Daughters*, in May of 1959.

Since then the Mermaid has mounted over 200 productions at the rate of ten a year. Many of these shows were written especially for its stage and some went on to the West End and subsequently became films, such as *Alfie* and *All In Good Time*.

Bernard Miles, now Lord Miles 'in recognition of his services to the theatre' must be admired equally for his creative work as for his tenacity in keeping the theatre open over all these years. The theatre's survival is a tribute to its reputation.

Bernard Miles as Falstaff. Some other famous roles of his were Iago in *Othello* and Long John Silver.

THE BARBICAN

The completion of the Barbican nearly quadrupled the city's permanent population, from 2,000 to over 7,000. The completion of the Barbican Centre in 1982 has given the City a further dimension in providing it not only with its own artistic centre but with a major conference centre as well.

The lively programme of the Barbican Centre offers not only the RSC, and the LSO when they are in residence, but presents a wide variety of attractions including jazz and light entertainment. An art gallery and a cinema also help to bring thousands of visitors to an area which was formerly deserted outside of business hours.

183

The London Symphony Orchestra

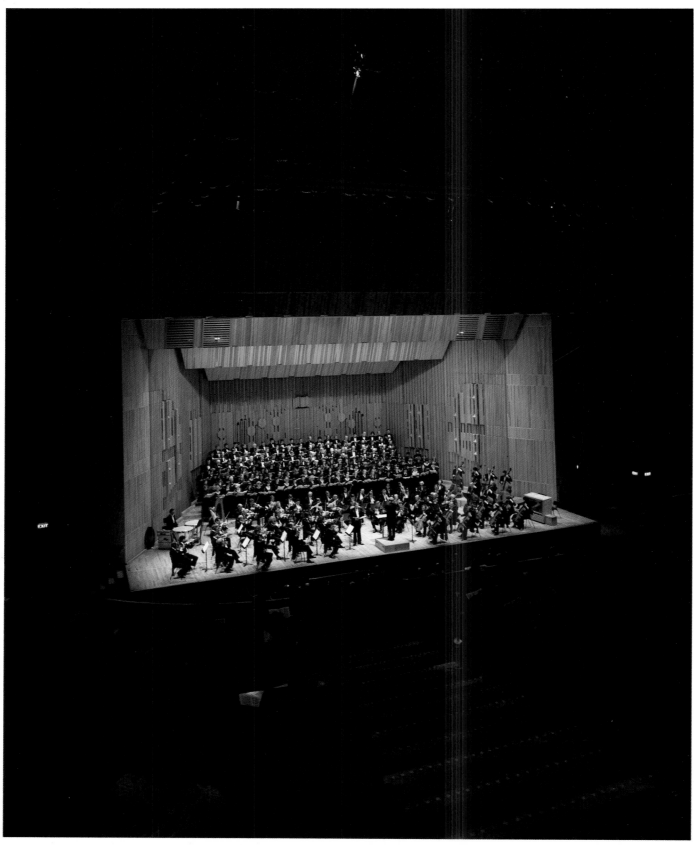

The LSO and the London Symphony Chorus conducted by Richard Hickox at the Barbican Hall.

The London Symphony Orchestra for the first
time now has a permanent home at the
Barbican Centre. Because of this the company
considers itself as the City resident orchestra
and its ties to the City are very strong.

In three seasons, March, July and November,
the company is now able to concentrate entirely
on its work and is free of the commercial work
formerly necessary to subsidize its
performances. This has been made possible
through grants, to which the City Corporation
is a party and individual sponsorships to which
City institutions subscribe.

Formed in 1904, the LSO is recognized as one of
the world's premier orchestras and under the
baton of Claudio Abbado, its principal
conductor, was able in its first season to attract
some of the world's finest soloists to the
Barbican Centre Hall.

Mark Elder, guest conductor, rehearsing the ▶
orchestra in a programme of American music,
including Harris, Bernstein, Ives and George
Gershwin.

The Royal Shakespeare Company

The Royal Shakespeare Company traces its history back to David Garrick's Jubilee at Stratford-upon-Avon in 1769, but only took its present name in 1960. Since the opening of the Shakespeare Memorial Theatre in 1879, the company has won worldwide acclaim for its Shakespeare productions, but over the years the company has also successfully staged numerous other works, resulting in a string of national and international awards.

The RSC's move to the Barbican Centre gives it two theatres, one a full-sized auditorium seating 1,150 and The Pit, a small studio space with flexible seating of around 200.

The design of the RSC's Barbican Theatre was the result of a uniquely close collaboration between Peter Hall, then Artistic Director, and John Bury, then Head of Design of the RSC, with Peter Chamberlin, the architect. The interior finishes were arrived at through a further collaboration between Trevor Nunn, Peter Chamberlin and, later, Christof Bon. Patrick Donnell was also an RSC Barbican Consultant and James Sargant is the RSC's Barbican Administrator.

Trevor Nunn, (left) Artistic Director since 1968 and Terry Hands, Joint Artistic Director with him since 1978 are the two men responsible for overall artistic direction of the RSC. They are joined by ten Associate Directors, two Resident Directors and Guest Directors. Mr Nunn, together with John Caird, recently directed the hugely successful *Nicholas Nickleby*. The show featuring 175 characters played by forty actors with a running time of just under eight and a half hours, was a sell-out in the West End and on Broadway. Terry Hands is best known for his staging of the eight plays in Shakespeare's history cycle from *Richard II* to *Richard III*.

A Midsummer Night's Dream, directed by Ron Daniels, was one of the Shakespeare plays presented by the company in its first season at the Barbican Theatre.

Joseph Marcel as Puck.

◄Juliet Stevenson, seen here as Hippolyta, Queen of the Amazons in Shakespeare's *A Midsummer Night's Dream*, directed by Ron Daniels, with the Changeling, played by Massimo Mezzofonti, also played the role of Titania, Queen of the Fairies, in the same production.

A view down Throgmorton Street past the Stock
Exchange, normally a hub of activity, shows the deserted
City on a Sunday afternoon. On the Thames only a
luxury yacht, anchored at Tower Pier, provides any life.

All photographs by Jacques Lowe except
page 39 The photographs of the Crown Jewels are reproduced under Crown copyright
with the permission of Her Majesty's Stationery Office.
pages 92/93 courtesy Gerrard & National
page 128 Goldfixing Barnett Saidman, Gold Harry Redl both of Camera Press
page 181 Forbes Nelson

The author wishes to thank the many generous men and women who gave of their time
and trust to allow photographs to be taken and information to be revealed without stint.

Special thanks are due Roger Gibbs of Gerrard & National, James Hambro of
Hambros Bank, Christopher Reeves of Morgan Grenfell & Co., Stanislaw
Ciechanowski of Morgan Guaranty Trust Company, Peter de Roos and Barret Petty of
Saudi International Bank as well as Mrs Marshall of the Bank of England, Tony Hughes
of the Stock Exchange, Brian Jones of Lloyds Bank, Frank Atkins of Lloyd's of London
and David Lamb of BP.

Mr Alan Davis of Armitage & Norton, Colonel Thacker of the Old Bailey, Dean
Webster of St Paul's Cathedral, William Hunt of the HAC, Michael Wakeford of the
Mercers' Company, Sir Peter Vanneck of the Fishmongers' Company, Lt. Col. Cowe of
the Armourers' and Brasiers' Company, Major O'Leary of the Apothecaries' Society and
Peter Wood and Adrian King of the City Corporation Public Relations Office also are
due special thanks.

I wish to thank Adrian Scrope for his sure and knowledgeable guidance on this book
since the very beginning and finally Ian Kalinowski, my assistant on many of the
photographs, Adrian Ensor, my black and white printer and Gary Grant and Roy
Trevelion of Namara Features must be thanked for their work in production and lay out
assistance and David Elliott of Quartet Books for his tremendous enthusiasm.

Jim Beach knows how I feel about his total commitment, but it is expressed here once
more and of course Naim Attallah's belief in this book is most important of all and my
thanks go to him for making it possible in the first place. Jacques Lowe.

DOMINE DIRIGE NOS